# The Challenge of the Able Child

# The Challenge of the Able Child

## Second Edition

David George

**David Fulton Publishers**

London

David Fulton Publishers Ltd
Ormond House, 26–27 Boswell Street, London WC1N 3JD

First published in Great Britain by David Fulton Publishers in 1992
Reprinted 1994, 1995
Second Edition published in Great Britain by David Fulton Publishers 1997

Note: The right of David George to be identified as the author of this work has been asserted by him in accordance with the Copyright, Designs and Patents Act 1988.

Copyright © David George

British Library Cataloguing in Publication Data

A catalogue record for this book is available from the British Library

ISBN 1–85346–346–9

Typeset by FSH Limited, London
Printed in Great Britain by The Cromwell Press Ltd, Melksham

# Contents

# Preface

It is a pleasure to have the opportunity to update and amend the book with the production of this second edition. The education of able children has moved on considerably, and this is reflected in the text, with many additions, updates in computer technology, new resources and an expanded bibliography.

There are so many new initiatives in education that it is extremely difficult for busy teachers and parents to keep up to date with what is happening. Teachers are supposed to be *au fait* with multi-ethnic education, equal opportunities, information technology, the National Curriculum and testing, changing examination systems, ever-changing course content, the home and environment, and the hidden curricula that children encounter. Here I am suggesting, in addition, that teachers should be very conscious of our more able children and the number that are underachieving at school.

Meeting the needs of able children has become the topic of widespread debate. A great deal of time, energy and money has been spent on children with other special needs, whereas the needs of children of high ability have been relatively neglected. The more rigorous and frequent monitoring of schools that has come about through OFSTED inspections has sharpened the focus in this area at last. Educational reforms and HMI reviews have set the framework in which this debate has moved forward.

I maintain that many, though not all, gifted and talented children have special needs and special problems. They also have special, sometimes immense, talent to give to society. We owe it to them to help cultivate their abilities and to society to help prepare tomorrow's leaders and talent. More able children are the most precious natural resource and one that must not be squandered. The survival and achievements of the human species owe much to one characteristic – a capacity for creative problem solving. This ability to find new answers to problems remains a vital one. A major objective of education for the more able is to recognise and foster this special ability. Unfortunately, the pursuit of this, and related objectives is often plagued with confusion, misconception, doubtful assumptions, exaggerated claims and a lack of communication.

It is the right of all children to go as far and as fast as they can along every dimension of the school curriculum without any brakes being put on them. Therefore, every child is entitled to the best programme, the most attentive care, and the greatest love and respect.

With this in mind, it is still reasonable to talk about groups of children who collectively have special needs but are not well served by what is provided, even by what is well provided, to typical or average learners. Of course, even the idea of typical average children must be regarded with care. The important question is this: are very bright, more able, gifted, talented children – call them what you may – systematically different from others in ways that might suggest educational change and adaptation? If we can identify some of these characteristics, then we should be able to justify special recognition and support for these children.

In addition to these goals, a denial of the legitimate aspirations of individuals must have special consequences. There is evidence that some of these children who are not recognised and supported become involved in crime and turn to delinquency. The need to nurture the whole child emphasised in this book signals an educationally enlightened approach to the question of gifted and able children, in contrast to many earlier works which were concerned only with the identification of educational potential as measured by 'convergent' intelligence tests. The approach here is firmly rooted in the more constructive multidimensional view of intelligence. This entails assisting students who are able to take self-initiated action and who are capable of intelligent choice, independent learning and problem solving. This will also help to maximise learning and individual development and to minimise boredom, confusion and frustration. It will encourage them to realise their contributions to themselves and to society as a whole.

Although this book is directed primarily at teachers, it should be a useful aid for other professionals and parents in identifying more able children and becoming more comfortable with them. It also aims to assist teachers to become more patient and observant in the classroom, thus giving them a knowledge base on which to work in defining their objectives and providing for these children. Finally, the book is intended to raise the awareness of teachers and parents to the fact that there are children underachieving in our schools and therefore not fulfilling their considerable potential.

This book may or may not change the minds of critics who feel that special education for the gifted is unfair, undemocratic or elitist. The virtues listed above, plus the argument that a true democracy includes full individual opportunity, may not breach their well-intentioned defences, but I hope they will go some way to dispel the myths that have grown up with this movement.

Importantly, the book does not ignore the special identification and programme needs of female gifted students or culturally different, economically disadvantaged, disabled or underachieving students whom many schools do not adequately accommodate. The book falls into two large sections, the first being designed to set the stage for the remainder. In order to discuss intelligently what should be done for our more able children in the educational system, we must firstly describe who we are talking about, and understand the special needs and characteristics of these young people and how to identify them more accurately. The second part of the book looks primarily at the provision for more able children and strategies for teaching them.

I would like to express my thanks to numerous colleagues who have supported the writing of this book: Dr Richard Alexander of School Scene who contributed much of the section on the assessment of intelligence, Alan Conchie for his update on Computer Technology, Caroline Jones for her contribution to the section on psychomotor talent and Sue Leyden for providing details of case studies. Several colleagues have given permission to quote from their writing, including those from schools where I have worked and where they are now identifying and supporting gifted and talented children. Pauline Vernon not only produced impressive typed work, but also provided me with calm support. Members of NACE, both teachers and students, contributed in many ways through discussions and anecdotes about these children and their invaluable experiences with them. I continue to learn from them. My apologies to those I have inadvertently left out or not acknowledged in the text.

In this book it is my hope that all of you who care about gifted individuals will find much that will aid you to discover the excitement, challenge and pleasure of being with these special children as they share the process of growing up. The waste of human potential is tragic for the community, for the world, but especially for the child. The concerto never written, the scientific discovery never made, the political compromise never found – they all carry heavy costs. Thomas Gray notes this loss in his *Elegy Written in a Country Churchyard*:

> Full many a flower is born to blush unseen
> And waste its sweetness on the desert air.

David George,
Northampton
December, 1996

# CHAPTER 1

# What's in a Name?

The gifted and talented come in a tremendous variety of shapes and sizes and are clearly not a homogeneous group. (Harry Passow)

Who are we talking about? Definitions abound and create much confusion. Anyone who takes the trouble to delve into the mass of published material on this subject is likely to be startled, if not confused, by the variety of terms used to describe very able children and the various criteria used to define them. Yet defining 'gifted' and 'talented' is an extremely important matter and surprisingly complicated. Many people still discuss giftedness or talent as if they constitute a syndrome or a set of recognisable characteristics. These are best seen as umbrella terms for individuals with a wide variety of special abilities. In some areas we hesitate to use the words 'gifted' and 'talented', but we shall do so because current English usage does not use these terms in the Biblical sense. Indeed, the parable of the talents in the New Testament is a very sad story because the third person buried his talents, so here was our first underachiever! The gifted are certainly not a homogeneous group and the search for general characteristics of giftedness has not been fruitful, except where a restricted definition has been used. I would suggest that we seek out what represents gifted behaviour in the fields of human endeavour in which we are interested, describe under what conditions such behaviour will emerge and identify ways of developing such behaviour. This will help us get away from pseudo-scientific labelling of children. But, for teachers, the term 'intellectually underserved' has some value. It indicates that the targets of our concern are those who have special learning abilities that have not been matched with an appropriate programme. Thus the identification process involves the study of not only the child's learning characteristics but also the learning environment.

To some people the concept of giftedness means the skills of an outstanding athlete, artist or musician, while for others it encompasses the work of a promising mathematician, scientist, writer or poet. Its application to levels of achievement may also vary from 'above average' to 'outstanding'. What is required is a working definition which can serve two purposes: provide an agreed statement to facilitate discussion and enable a positive response to anyone requiring further clarification of their ideas of exceptional ability. A clear working definition must lie between the two extremes, being neither too specific – it should not be so narrowly conceived that some children of exceptional ability are excluded, nor so broad and that no clear guidance is given.

The particular definition adopted by a school in its policy for gifted and talented children is vitally important because it will determine who is selected for any special programme. Further, there is a danger that one's definition and consequent identification methods will discriminate against such special populations as the poor, minority groups, the disabled underachievers and even some female students.

Renzulli et al. (1981) noted that a definition of giftedness must

(1)   be based on research about characteristics of gifted children;
(2)   provide guidance in the identification process;
(3)   give direction and be logically related to programming practices;
(4)   be capable of generating research that would test the validity of the definition.

The following terms are just some that I have encountered: 'able', 'more able', 'exceptional', 'talented', 'superior', 'gifted', 'higher educational potentials', 'more receptive learners', 'more capable learners' and 'higher academic potentials'. These terms may or may not refer to the same or similar groups of children. There are obvious dangers in making generalisations about any group of people and this is no less true when talking about very able children.

These observations suggest that, although the notion of the gifted and talented child has been generally recognised, the need for a more exact definition is a new phenomenon in our educational system. But why has it taken so long to realise this need even when society recognises the general notion of the gifted?

One can respond by citing the following reasons. Firstly, identifying the gifted child through performance of the given task was sufficient. The educational system itself was felt to be good enough to identify the gifted. That is to say, nobody was interested in discovering the gifted children in the early stages of their education. Secondly, there seems to be a cultural factor in the sense that to be gifted is to be different, and the idea of an individual being different from the others within society should not be encouraged. Having made these observations, it is fair to want to know what has prompted the sudden urge to have more precise definitions of the gifted child. Our society has come to realise the importance of having a deeper understanding of gifted children and, if possible, of identifying their essential characteristics.

This new interest has been influenced by the following factors, among others. Firstly, psychologists have become increasingly interested in the functioning of the human mind. In their efforts to understand how the mind works, these professionals have discovered that some individuals are endowed with very little potential to perform certain tasks which most average children find rather

> The term "gifted" implies receiving something for nothing, and it is difficult to garner sympathy for someone so apparently blessed.' (P. O. Rogne)
> Here are a number of **alternative terms** which could be used when referring to students who have the potential for excellence.
>
> PROMISING                                              CAPABLE
>   INTELLIGENT                               INDEPENDENT
>     POTENTIAL                      UNUSUAL THINKING
>       INQUISITIVE          EXCITED LEARNER
>             EMERGING TALENT
>     ACHIEVER                        RISK TAKERS
>     MOTIVATED                       INNOVATORS
>         HIGHLY ABLE            INSIGHTFUL
>   OUTSTANDING
>                                     SPONTANEOUS
>                          CHALLENGING AUTONOMOUS
>   CREATIVE                    ACCELERATED LEARNER
>       ADVANCED
>         FAST LEARNER
>           EXCEPTIONALLY BRIGHT
>   SELF-DIRECTED                            LEADER
>           'GOT WHAT IT TAKES'

easy to perform. Psychologists identified these children as needing to be treated differently from average children, but some felt it would be unfair to assess the intellectual performance of intellectually abnormal children even when we realise that the intellectual potential in the two groups is quite different. Nevertheless, there followed the establishment of special educational institutions, and specialist teachers and a great deal of money were provided to support this work. It is now a legal requirement to support children who are disabled, whether emotionally, physically or intellectually. Later it was realised that by concentrating on the needs of disabled children, educators were dealing with only one end of the normal distribution curve of children's ability. The other end of the spectrum consisted of those children who seemed to be endowed with performance potential that was over and above that possessed by the average child.

Secondly, education has been recognised as an inalienable right for all individuals. Consequently, governments are expected to make sure that both the normal and the abnormal are presented with the most relevant education. This also calls for the most appropriate method of teaching these important but different groups of individuals.

Thirdly, in our modern societies certain specialised services are identified from time to time. These services may, for example, require people with very high intellectual abilities. In such circumstances, society has a duty to identify those individuals who are endowed with the requisite abilities. A case in point is that some countries have now established educational institutions for students with high potential in science and mathematics (to help in international competition in space programmes) and sport (international sporting events).

Fourthly, the belief that education is an inalienable right implies that the cost of running schools is very high for any government. It has also been discovered that children with more than normal potential ability take a shorter time to learn certain tasks than average and disabled children. If governments are able to identify children with higher than normal potential abilities, they may end up spending *less* money on them.

Fifthly, some social scientists have discovered that children will engage in anti-social behaviour for lack of anything better to do. These are children who, because of their high potential ability, take a shorter time to accomplish certain tasks than the average child. In a classroom situation, such children may resort to making mischief because they are often idle for some of the time. Thus, it will be important to identify these types of children in order to reduce anti-social behaviour in our school systems and in society at large.

Sixthly, scholars are interested to understand the nature of human beings, and particularly to establish the limits of their intellectual potential.

Finally, educationalists are agreed that it is every child's right to go as far and as fast as possible along every dimension of the school curriculum in order to reach their considerable potential, and that this is one of the major aims of education.

Now, if the reasons cited above can stand the test of time, then an attempt should be made to offer an appropriate definition of the gifted child. It is clear that one cannot identify a single purpose as the motivation for wanting to define terms. However, for every definition, some purposes are more pronounced than others. Thus, for this book, my main interest is to attempt to reduce the vagueness inherent in the term 'giftedness' as it is commonly used. If I register any measure of success towards this end, then I hope it will be of some use to teachers and parents, as well as to social workers, policy makers and researchers as they deliberate about the gifted and talented individuals in our society.

Discussion on the precise definition of gifted and talented children should begin rather humbly by examining some versions of the term 'gifted' advanced by scholars and other interested groups, led by Plato (*The Republic*). In his attempt to find a lasting solution regarding the best government in his Athenian city-state, Plato indicated that in any community there are three groups of people: the craftsmen, the civil servants and the philosophers. His classification was based on the potential endowment of intellectual abilities each class enjoyed. While the craftsmen were least endowed with intellectual abilities, the philosophers possessed the most. Plato then prescribed a system of education which would help to sort out who belonged to each group. Thus most people would drop out of the education system and only a small group would reach the apex. This small group consisted of individuals who were the best at handling dialectics, one of the most abstract and intellectually demanding subjects offered in the Athenian educational system of that day. It was from this small group that the king was to come.

Even if Plato never talked about 'the gifted' as such, it is plausible to infer the notion from the above general observations. If this is granted then one is likely to draw out certain features from the notion of giftedness adopted by Plato. Firstly, the gifted individual exhibits superior intellectual abilities. Secondly, the human abilities considered as gifts are also useful in the service of society in general. Thirdly, only a small percentage of the entire community is endowed with a particular gift. Finally, the potential gift is within an individual from birth, waiting to be developed.

The next definition of the gifted individual to be considered is given by Painter (1980), who states that

> The capabilities which go to make up giftedness are not absolute for all types of societies and stages of economic development. Those qualities which will be considered to represent 'gifts', even if that particular word is not used, will be the abilities which enable individuals to perform those functions which are the most highly prized in their respective communities or who are able to produce the type of artefact in great demand.

The quotation reinforces the observation made about Plato that giftedness refers to those superior abilities considered to be most worthwhile in the eyes of the community concerned. However, whereas Painter would consider any human ability as potentially a gift, Plato would so consider only intellectual abilities. It is also important to note the new feature in Painter's definition: that the values and priorities of a particular society will dictate which abilities are to be valued as 'gifts' within that society.

In a definition by Newland (1976) a gifted or talented child is one who shows consistent remarkable performance in any endeavour. This definition is consonant with the previous two, regarding as central the place that superior abilities and their usefulness enjoyed in the meaning of giftedness. But two rather subtle notions are floated here – that the superior abilities be demonstrated in the performance of the individual considered as gifted and, above that, that the superior performance be consistent in the particular individual. This caveat excludes from the definition those examples of exceptional achievement that occur by chance or in isolation. For example, the student who manages to be top of his or her class in a physics examination by scoring 90 per cent is not to be considered gifted just on the strength of this one particular performance.

Two more definitions of the gifted may be noted. On the one hand, a gift is said to imply something that is freely given and that, as a present, may be expected to be beneficial to the recipient (Painter, 1980). On the other hand, giftedness is said to be our own invention rather than something we discover; that it is what one society or another wants it to be and hence its conceptualisation can change over time and space (Sternberg and Davidson, 1986). Note that the first of the two definitions does add a new feature to the meaning of giftedness: that what is considered a gift should be of some worth from the perspective of the individual involved. However, what might concern a careful observer is the seemingly antagonistic stance that each of the above definitions takes regarding the origin of what is considered as a gift in an individual. Thus, whereas one definition emphasises that gifts are freely given to an individual (Plato concurs in this), the other stresses that gifts can be regarded as human contrivances. How do we get ourselves out of this difficulty?

It seems to me that rather than the two definitions conflicting over the origin of talent, they each constitute distinct, but not inconsistent, features within an overall definition. Thus, one stresses that human abilities that are considered as gifts are bestowed upon individuals freely and naturally. The other, however, stresses the fact that the decision as to which abilities qualify as gifts falls squarely on the students themselves. In a nutshell, although we are not the originators of human potential abilities, whatever abilities are developed and eventually qualify as human gifts depend strictly on human decisions. These crucial decisions will of course be influenced by which talents are currently in demand in a particular society. In addition, they are greatly influenced by teachers, parents and the ethos of schools.

There is yet another type of definition of the gifted which seems to be rather different from those discussed above. According to psychologists, the gifted are considered to be those two hundred superior individuals in a thousand in a given ability; the extremely gifted are those ten superior individuals out of a thousand in a given ability; and the genius as the one top individual in a thousand in a given ability. This definition emphasises certain features that are also noted in one way or another in definitions cited earlier. For example, giftedness involves any human ability, be it intellectual, physical or moral, and regardless of whether it is useful or not. However, the definition does highlight the fact that a superiority involving a single ability would qualify an individual to be regarded as gifted.

From the discussion so far, the following features have emerged as possible contributions to a definition of giftedness:

- superior human abilities;
- superior intellectual abilities;
- natural human abilities;

- superior potential human abilities;
- superior human performance;
- consistent superior human performance;
- an intelligence quotient above 100 per cent;
- placement in the top two hundred in a homogeneous group of one thousand students.

The greatest challenge now is to find out which of the above features can be considered as legitimate in a definition of giftedness and which we cannot accept, especially when some contradictions seem implied.

A quick perusal of the features listed suggests some agreement as to what is central in a definition of a gifted individual. For instance, there seems to be common agreement that natural superior human abilities are part of what is understood as 'giftedness'. This agreement is either explicitly or implicitly expressed. The next aspect is the worthwhileness or utility of the human abilities that are regarded as gifts. Here the degree of agreement is high, but not unanimous. However, it seems to me that even those who do not endorse eventual worthwhileness as a required aspect of giftedness are doing so indirectly. This is because the concept of worthwhileness is already embedded within the meaning of 'superiority' in the phrase 'superior human abilities'. Thus, if for the moment we take these features as central to the meaning of giftedness, then we can say that a gifted individual is one endowed with superior natural abilities which are regarded as worthwhile. But is this a satisfactory definition of 'the gifted'?

A further critical study of various definitions reveals that the gifted individual is always in a minority in a homogeneous group of people. If this observation is correct, then we could improve our earlier definition by saying that a gifted person is that individual within a small percentage of a homogeneous group of people who is endowed with one or more superior natural abilities which are regarded as worthwhile. Though this improved definition seems to take care of the *common* features in defining giftedness many questions have still to be raised regarding the features listed previously.

The way out of this problem is to note that the suggested definition provides just the bare minimum. Beyond that, each particular definition of the gifted must take other factors into account. For instance, those who are interested in the accurate measurement of superior human abilities are likely to emphasise the *performance* aspects of such abilities. On the other hand, educators and others are likely to define an individual as gifted from the perspective of their *potential* abilities. This is to say that although the two groups acknowledge the central position occupied by superior human abilities in defining giftedness, each group tends to emphasise a different aspect. Furthermore, there are those, like Plato, who equate superior human abilities with intellectual abilities only.

In the Western world it has been an established tradition to reward intellectual abilities more than any other human abilities. Today, that picture is gradually changing so that, for example, superior athletes are being recognised as among the gifted and rewarded accordingly.

As the reader can see, there is no one theory-based definition of 'gifted' and 'talented' that is universally accepted and that will fit all programmes and contexts for our children. The general use of these terms is ambiguous and inconsistent; for example, it is common and acceptable nowadays to use them interchangeably, as when we describe the same person as being a 'gifted musician' or a 'talented musician'. Two well-known researchers in this field, Renzulli (Renzulli, 1988; Renzulli et al., 1981) and Treffinger (Treffinger and Renzulli, 1986), prefer the phrase 'gifted behaviour' to describe aptitudes which can be developed in certain students in certain circumstances.

Ogilvie (1973) prefers a broad definition which is flexible and inclusive. He suggests that to be gifted is to be outstanding in general or specific abilities in a relatively broad or narrow field of endeavour. Within this broad definition, he suggests six areas for consideration: physical talent; mechanical ingenuity; visual and performing abilities; outstanding leadership and social awareness; creativity; and high intelligence. Ogilvie goes further, and from his research states that 3 per cent of English children are broadly gifted across the curriculum, but 36 per cent have individual talents, and this may be a way out of our dilemma of finding the right definition. Gagne (1985) concludes that gifts as opposed to talent should reflect the psychological distinction between ability and performance. That is, the gifted person is one who is distinctly above average in intellectual, creative and other areas of general ability, whereas talent refers to distinctly above-average performance in specific activities, such as mathematics, music or art.

Ogilvie's definition is very similar to that of the US Office of Education (Marland, 1972) which employs a multi-talent approach and is one of the most commonly used definitions. It states that

> gifted and talented children are those identified by professionally qualified persons who, by virtue of outstanding abilities, are capable of high performance. These are children who require differentiated educational programs and services beyond those normally provided by the regular school program in order to realize their contribution to self and society.

It states further that children capable of high performance include those with demonstrated achievement and/or potential in any of the following areas: general intellectual ability; specific academic aptitude; creative or productive thinking; leadership ability; visual and performing arts; and psychomotor ability. This definition has great appeal because it recognises not only high general intelligence but gifts in specific academic areas as well as in the arts, and such human attributes as creativity, leadership and psychomotor abilities.

It further recognises that gifted and talented students require differentiated educational programmes beyond those normally provided for the majority of children. It also recognises the two basic aims of gifted children programmes, which are to help individual gifted and talented children to develop their potential and to provide society with educated people who are creative leaders and problem-solvers. It is also to be noted that demonstrated achievement and/or potential ability take into consideration underachieving students who may not be demonstrating their gifts and talents in school.

Later, in 1978, the US Congress revised Marland's definition, and psychomotor ability was excluded because artistic psychomotor talents such as dance could be included under the performing arts and talented students in sport were well provided for in schools. This is probably true in the Western world and increasingly elsewhere, because identifying able children in sport is prestigious for both school and country and, on the whole, these children are well provided for with extra coaching, equipment and a great deal of competition. In addition, they are encouraged and rewarded for their efforts. However, Treffinger and Renzulli (1986) said of this definition that the categories are frequently ambiguous, undefinable, overlapping and often adopted with no regard for their actual implications for identification or classroom teaching.

Increasingly, educators believe that gifted persons are those who make valuable contributions to society. Renzulli (1988) argues that gifted behaviour reflects an interaction between three basic components of human ability: above-average general or specific abilities, high levels of task commitment (motivation), and high levels of creativity. He believed that gifted and talented children are those possessing, or capable of developing, these traits and who apply them to any potentially valuable area of human performance. Taylor's (1978) multi-talent totem pole model raises our awareness that most students possess special skills and talents in some variety. But there is a serious problem here if one goes on to assume that all children are gifted. However, his broad definition of giftedness may be best viewed as an appropriate way to understand, perceive and teach all our children, and this book is about good practice in schools.

As a consequence of this discussion, it appears that vagueness is inevitable in seeking to define the gifted or talented person. The best we can do is to understand giftedness as clearly as we can and act accordingly for the benefit of our children. There is obviously no one final and agreed definition of 'gifted' and 'talented'. The definition applied to any special training programme for these children will determine selection criteria and procedures, and these, in turn, will reinforce the notions of giftedness and talent appropriate in the context.

As with so many definitions of exceptional students these notions are somewhat subjective. There is still considerable debate as to what constitutes outstanding ability or high performance capability. One could argue that almost all children are gifted or talented in some way; it is just a matter of finding the individual person's talent. Taylor (1978) maintained that virtually everyone has special strengths and theoretically, therefore, could be considered gifted or talented. Lloyd Spencer of Moi University, Kenya, at the first East African Conference on Gifted Education in 1991 said, 'one definition of a gifted child is a child who makes definitions of giftedness irrelevant'.

As there are currently over 200 different definitions of 'giftedness' and a proliferation of terms such as 'gifted', 'talented', 'more able', 'exceptional', 'marked aptitude', teachers should devise their own working definition. Each will inevitably be a generalisation, because all pupils are different. A definition based on the possession of a high score of general ability – say an IQ of 140 – is neither proven nor credible as we approach the year 2000. The Marland (1972) and Ogilvie (1973) definitions are similar and probably the best, but, in the context of Britain's National Curriculum, the following is worthy of serious consideration: gifted and talented children are those who are functioning at the upper end of a particular key stage or are one key stage ahead and who possess abilities so well developed and so far in advance of their peer group that a school has to provide additional learning experiences which develop, enhance and extend these abilities. The debate continues and the jury is still out!

## UNDERACHIEVEMENT

Before concluding this chapter the reader should consider the particular problem of the underachieving child. Creative and imaginative people are often not recognised by their contemporaries. In fact often they are not recognised by their teachers either. This is not a new phenomenon, as the following examples demonstrate:

*Noel Coward* 'When Noel was still two the doctor pronounced that his brain was much in advance of his body and advised that he should be left very quiet, that all his curls should be cut off and that he was to go to no parties'.

*David Bellamy* School report – 'Bellamy is a good fellow, is maturing well but is academically useless'.

*Roald Dahl* English report at 16 – 'The boy is an indolent and illiterate member of the class'.

*Albert Einstein* School report – 'mentally slow, unsociable and adrift forever in his foolish dreams'. Einstein, that gifted synthesiser of the time-space continuum, was four years old before he could speak and seven before he could read.

*Ted Allbery* He left school to go into a foundry and was told he was 'on the dust heap of life'. He started writing at 55 after a major upset in his personal life.

*Scott Hamilton* His growth was stunted at a very early age and he was a very sickly child. It was suggested he tried activities such as ice-skating. He became World Champion on four occasions.

*Dame Alicia Markova* She was taken to the doctor because she had flat feet. He suggested ballet!

*Stephen Wiltshire* 'A foolish wise one' (IQ 60). 'I have never seen in all my competition drawing such a talent that this child seems to have ... Stephen is possibly the best child artist in Britain' (Sir Hugh Casson).

*Issac Newton* One of our greatest scientists did poorly in high school.

*Beethoven* His music teacher once said of him, 'As a composer, he is hopeless'.

*Abraham Lincoln* Entered the Black Hawk War as a captain and came out as a private.

*Winston Churchill* Failed examinations.

These people were probably identified as underachievers in school or as misfits. The phenomenon of underachieving is both challenging and puzzling – puzzling in its complexities and challenging in the significance of the reversal of this costly syndrome. Space will not permit an extended discussion of this important subject, but the reader is referred to the excellent books by Nava Butler-Por (1987) and Sylvia Rimm (1989).

Gifted children are at high psychological risk in that their unique intellectual and creative abilities make them vulnerable to pressures at home and at school which may initiate underachievement. Underachievement is a discrepancy between a child's school performance and some index of his or her actual ability, or a performance in scholastic attainment which is substantially below predicted levels. Gardner (1961) states: 'the fact that a large number of American boys and girls failed to attain their full development must weigh heavily on our national conscience.' In England, numerous HMI reports give evidence from schools surveys that many young people fail to achieve their full potential. My definition of underachievement is based on test results which generally have their pitfalls and, in face of the dynamic nature of underachievement, are particularly problematic. Since many schools do not habitually administer intelligence and achievement tests, teachers should employ alternative methods of identification which utilise the resources available within the normal classroom situation. This information can be gleaned from various sources:

• understanding the behaviour and recognising the characteristics of underachievers;
• using diagnostic teaching methods;
• collecting relevant data (such as that available from children's records);
• consulting parents;
• enlisting professional help.

Studies of gifted underachievers have identified a set of typical characteristics. These can be categorised into three levels in terms of their causes and symptoms. The most important characteristic, which appears to be at the root of most underachievement problems, is low self-esteem and this seems to lead to the secondary characteristic of academic avoidance behaviour. This in turn leads to poor study habits, unmastered skills, poor peer-acceptance and lack of concentration in school.

Teachers and parents are advised to observe children over several weeks to determine if a child possesses any of the following characteristics. If a child exhibits ten or more, it is recommended that an individual intelligence test be administered to establish whether the child is gifted but underachieving.

### Profile of an underachiever

- poor test performance;
- orally knowledgeable but poor in written work;
- superior comprehension and retention of concepts when interested;
- apparently bored;
- achieving below expectations in basic subjects;
- restless or inattentive;
- daily work often incomplete or poorly done;
- dislikes practice work;
- absorbed in a private world;
- tactless and impatient of slower minds;
- prefers friendship with older pupils or adults;
- excessively self-critical;
- unable to make good relationships with peer group and teachers;
- emotionally unstable – low self-esteem, withdrawn and sometimes aggressive;
- has wide range of interests and possibly an area of real expertise.

Parenting the gifted child will be discussed later in the book, but it is relevant to mention here that research shows worse overall achievement for boys in father-absent homes and worse maths and problem-solving skills for both sexes in such homes. Successful career mothers serve as effective models for achieving girls. Parents have a significant part to play in identifying these children, but their main role is to provide support and encouragement for the development of as wide a range of skills as possible. At the same time, it is important for children to receive the right balance between encouragement and correction. Children should be helped to avoid manipulating their environments instead of making a real effort.

The following characteristics foster underachievement in our children:

- inflexibility and rigidity in schools;

- stress on external evaluation;
- a perceived lack of genuine respect from parents or teachers for each individual child;
- a competitive social climate;
- dominance of criticism from both home and school;
- an unrewarding curriculum;
- a lack of opportunity to communicate what they have learnt;
- work too easy or tasks lacking in purpose.

As I have briefly discussed, the underachieving gifted child often continues to underachieve because home, school or peer group reinforce that underachievement. Lack of motivation and deficiency in some of the skills required for achieving full potential can induce the habit of working below the child's ability, affecting both educational success and eventual career achievement.

The remedy for underachievement is best summed up in Rimm's model (1989), the implementation of which involves the collaboration of school and family:

- The first step in the underachievement reversal process is an assessment that involves the co-operation of the educational psychologist, teachers and parents (see Assessment Policy, pp.16–17).
- Communication between parents and teachers is an important component of the cure for underachievers. This should include a discussion of assessed abilities and achievements, as well as formal and informal evaluations of the child's expression of dependence or dominance in order to avoid reinforcing these problem patterns. This may again involve an educational psychologist and at least a wise school counsellor or tutor group leader.
- Changing expectations is often difficult because sometimes both parents and teachers have low expectations of children, owing to various factors. However, it is important to underachieving children that parents and teachers are honestly able to express belief in their potential for greater achievement.

*[Bloom's (1985) studies of talent development found that parents of research neurologists and mathematicians always expected their children to be very good students. In contrast, the author undertook some work in a very poor part of Liverpool in a solid but dilapidated late-Victorian school, overlooking the Mersey and flanked by council houses and back-to-back terraces. Pupils from this school come from the immediate locality with its poor housing, high crime rate and chronic unemployment. A quarter of the children belong to ethnic minorities. The overall problem is the low aspirations of many of the pupils and low expectations from parents. Evidence for this is that less than 4 per cent of pupils get four or more A to*

*C Grade GCSEs and only one in four stays into the sixth form: eleven percentage points below the national average.*

*Sir Christopher Ball, who is leading a study for the Royal Society of Arts into why so many young people drop out of education at 16, says 'there is nothing wrong with the English system of education and we must guard against the idea that young people are either stupid or sunk in low aspirations'. Young people in areas such as that described above get their negative attitude to education from their parents – working-class dropouts beget working-class dropouts – and even more intensively from their peers. However, in the school described there are still steps being made and excellent staff doing their best to improve this school environment that expects and values high achievement.]*

- A critical turning point for the underachieving child is the discovery of a model for identification.

  *[As noted above, Bloom's biographical research with highly intelligent students shows that parents model the values and life styles of successful achievers in the talent area. When a parent is perceived as competent and strong, pleased with their job and willing to permit their children to master tasks independently, then this makes for an ideal family environment for a gifted child. Since this ideal family situation is rarely provided for the gifted underachiever, then parents and teachers need to help the student find a good model for identification. This often is the class or subject teacher, or a good outside mentor who has been matched to the individual child very carefully.]*

- The behaviour discussed in the first step above will identify some of the areas where reinforcement at home and school will help the underachieving child. These may take the form of rewards which are meaningful to the child and should be within the value system of parents and child, as well as being within the capabilities of teachers to administer.

Above all, these children need patience, dedication and warm, encouraging support from both parents and teachers. Butler-Por (1987) concludes that we should adopt a multi-dimensional approach to the problems of underachieving children, providing an appropriate educational environment in the classroom and utilising teaching methods capable of answering children's needs. These can contribute towards reversing underachievement in young children of all ability levels.

Since teachers often encounter difficulties in recognising both the diversity of potential and the specific needs of underachievers in their classes, this book encourages both them and the parents of the children in their charge to improve their understanding of the capabilities, needs and behaviour of children, so that they can initiate the appropriate intervention and plan the kind of educational environment and learning experiences capable of breaking the cycle of failure in some children.

As we learn more about the characteristics of gifted and talented children, we find that a significant proportion of them have been overlooked. These students would demonstrate their abilities if they were given circumstances and opportunities that enable them to emerge.

Students with 'hidden talents' are likely to be found in the following groups:

- those from low socio-economic backgrounds,
- female students who, for example, are under-represented in higher levels of maths and science,
- male students who under-participate in language and humanities,
- students with learning difficulties or specific disabilities,
- students with poor self-concept or inhibiting social or economic problems,
- students from homes where there are low expectations and/or negative attitudes towards schools and teachers,
- students from ethnic minority groups with a different culture and language but with special talents,
- students whose education has been disrupted for various reasons, such as family mobility,
- students who have particularly divergent thinking and are non-conforming.

Harvey and Steeley (1984) administered a battery of tests at a correctional centre and found that 18 per cent of the participants were gifted. They also noted that the pattern of abilities was not consistent with classroom-related tasks. Clearly the need to identify special categories of giftedness is one of the greatest challenges facing those of us interested in this field. Gifted children from different cultures are also difficult to identify. Coleman (1985) noted that the number of gifted students from non-white, non-middle-class, non-urban backgrounds is disproportionally low. Identification is difficult because such students typically score lower than average on traditional tests of intelligence and achievement. It is hard to find research to indicate why this is the case. Some say that the tests themselves are biased, whereas others support the idea that these children score low because of the lack of opportunity to develop and grow intellectually. Here is a challenge for further research, but it is apparent that students from minority groups or impoverished backgrounds have the potential if given the opportunity to achieve highly.

The education of gifted girls has historically been largely ignored. In the workforce, women continue to be under-represented in the most traditional male professions and salaries are comparatively poor. No country in the world can afford to undervalue 50 per cent of its national potential. Although in many countries the gifts and talents of girls are being recognised, there is still a long way to go. Historically the main problem is the home–career conflict and, although there is no easy solution, some women decide in advance to compromise a career to fit husband and family needs.

Peer attitudes and expectations often depress female achievement and school expectations often reward male independence, confidence and aggressiveness but reward female conformity. There is some evidence to suggest that all-girl classes and all-girl schools may help some girls to take leadership positions, as well as to study courses they might otherwise avoid, such as mathematics and science.

This special cultural problem of the underachievement of women requires individuals and societies to rethink cultural values in order to support the development of women. The rewards to individual girls and to society as a whole will make the effort most worthwhile.

## A GOOD SCHOOL ASSESSMENT POLICY

Effective assessment is a means of motivating, developing and recognising student achievement and self-esteem and of providing constructive feedback to all concerned. Teachers continually assess children by a variety of methods and not just by testing.

### The aims of assessment:

- to involve students in review and target-setting to maximise encouragement, motivation and progress;
- to provide an accurate representation of student achievement for effective use in both setting student targets and evaluating and planning teaching programmes;
- to provide regular and accurate information for students, parents, teachers and governors;
- to celebrate success and avoid underachievement.

### The assessment process

- is an integral part of the school year reflecting the requirements of the National Curriculum and other syllabuses;
- is a manageable part of the learning process;
- takes account of differentiation;
- is founded in knowledge of both the criteria for assessments and routes of progression;
- is based upon understanding of the assessment procedures;
- is founded in student self-assessment incorporating reflection, review, recording and target-setting.

### The assessment structure

- is based upon agreed departmental policy in which there is standardisation of approach based upon
  - departmental portfolios of exemplars of agreed levels

– clearly defined marking criteria and comments
– accurate and easy-to-use assessment guidelines.

## The assessment recording system

- involves teachers and students in a manageable, accessible structure;
- gives a clear and accurate indicator of student attainment;
- records achievements and levels to indicate progression from year to year, key stage to key stage, school to school;
- responds to internal school and external educational demands.

## The assessment reporting process

- should be regular, rapid, clear, concise, constructive, informative, honest and accurate;
- should identify strengths and weaknesses;
- should involve and be valued by students and parents for its effective, encouraging, personal content.

---

**Exercise for teachers and parents**
# What is achievement?
Read through the *descriptions of achievement* listed below and put them in order of importance, giving the most important number 1, the next important 2 and so on.

- attainment and test scores, eg SATs, end of unit tests, etc.
- public exam results
- expected public exam results
- continuous assessment scores
- continuous assessment feedback
- "in the top set'
- teacher assessment of pupil's learning and progress
- pupil's assessment of learning and progress
- opportunities for pupils to use what they know or can do
- opportunities for pupils to have a broad education
- personal development, e.g. confidence
- any other (please state)

Now do the same with these *processes that affect achievement:*

- choice for pupil
- relevance of the curriculum for pupils
- breadth of the curriculum
- teacher's style of instruction
- teacher's clear presentation
- pupil's relationship with teacher
- teacher's expectation of individual pupils
- behaviour of pupils in class
- quality of school/staff relationships
- quality of resources and environment
- quality of teacher's relationship with parents
- quality of school's relationship with parents
- any other (please state)

---

# CHAPTER 2

# The Characteristics of Gifted and Talented Children

> Children never give a wrong answer . . . they merely answer a different question.
> It is our job to find out which one they answered correctly and honour what they
> know.
> (Bob Samples)

Having discussed at some length a definition of gifted and talented children, for the remainder of this book I shall use the following working definition: gifted students are those with a potential to exhibit superior performance across a wide range of areas of endeavour; talented students are those with a potential to exhibit superior performance in one area of endeavour. These areas are recognised as being intellectual/academic, creative, social or leadership, as well as psychomotor.

It is important to realise that gifted and talented students are not a homogeneous group. They do not share the same traits or characteristics, but rather exhibit a wide range of individual differences. No single trait constitutes giftedness. Gifted and talented students often exhibit superior abilities and task commitment, though not necessarily in pro-social ways or within the school curriculum. Both gifted and talented students are frequently creative. Children's gifts and talents may become apparent at different stages of their lives. A child may exhibit talents in one area, for example art or music, or in a combination of areas. Gifted and talented children are present in all groups in society, including those requiring remediation in certain subject areas.

It is also important to recognise which characteristics these children do not have. It is not only the general public who have misconceptions about gifted and talented children, but also many educators. There has been much misinformation about the characteristics of these individuals, and particularly about personality characteristics. Many people assume that these children are in some way different. Case studies frequently include the adjectives 'neurotic', 'socially inept' and 'lonely'. Research, however, has repudiated these descriptions. Most of the myths are based on stereotypes of gifted students as a group. Obviously each gifted or talented student will have different strengths, personality and characteristics, just like all children. Lock and Jay (1987), for example, noted that gifted girls reported a more positive self-concept than did their non-gifted peers, whereas gifted boys reported a lower self-concept.

Lewis Terman, who was actively involved in the development of the Stanford-Binet Intelligence Scale, followed 1,500 gifted individuals over 30 years, and some of that work continues today. All these people had IQs above 140, which is a very high cut-off point. The data indicated that these individuals were well adjusted, had superior physical characteristics and made a successful transition into the working world, frequently becoming leaders in their professions. The data also indicated that, as children, they were advanced in reading, language usage, arithmetic reasoning, science, literature and the arts. However, the gifted children's superiority was less marked in certain areas such as spelling and history (Terman and Oden, 1959). It was also apparent that not all these children had the same strengths and weaknesses. More recently, Freeman (1991) traced 169 young people from a previous study of 210 5–15 year olds. These studies have done more than most to remove the myths and stereotypes from the contentious and emotive subject of gifted children and their education.

Recent research presents a fascinating picture of how different kinds of homes and schools deal with intellectually outstanding children, and how the children themselves react both to their unusual abilities and to their education. Many of these children are now at university, but others have dropped out after choosing unsuitable courses, or, in the case of working-class students, facing astonishing class snobbery at the prestige universities. Others are unemployed, and some have suffered from considerable depression and loneliness. Many had received virtually no advice about educational choices and careers, even though, being good at almost everything, choices were difficult. One of the problems was that the children were really offered only one target, and that was to go to university. Schools tried to eke out every ounce of academic achievement, whereas the children needed a wide range of opportunities outside the academic curriculum, because they had potential for many things.

This situation is not perhaps as stressful as might first be thought. George (1990) sees a superior sense of humour in most gifted children following quite naturally from their ability to think quickly and make connections, and this is confirmed by Clark (1988) and others. Their humour often appears in art, creative writing and social interaction, and is a part of their general confidence. In addition, when considering a definition of gifted individuals, creativity always enters into the picture. Many discoveries, inventions and artistic creations are the result of 'fooling around' with ideas and playing with possibilities.

## CHARACTERISTICS OF THE CREATIVE CHILD

An area in which gifted and talented children often excel is creativity. Brighter children tend to do more creative work and score high on creativity tests. However, above an IQ of about 100, the relationship drops to virtually nothing, which means that the creative and intelligent characteristics of these children might be quite independent of each other. Creativity is an extremely difficult concept to define and measure. It is certainly something to do with perception, intuition, consciousness, thinking skills and problem solving, as well as the use of our senses. The term, in fact, has multiple meanings and can be defined quite differently by a variety of people (Klein, 1982).

It is most important to distinguish between intelligence and creativity when we select students for special programmes in school. It is all too easy for teachers to select those who conform, are prompt, neat and 'teacher pleasers', rather than creative children who are less conforming. Some of the earlier and most interesting work in this area was conducted by Paul Torrance (1977), who devised tests of creative thinking (which will be discussed in Chapter 3). Torrance produced a checklist of the characteristics of creative students, which include:

- skills in group activities,
- the ability to express emotions easily,
- a keen sense of humour,
- originality and persistence in problem solving,
- curiosity,
- high energy levels,
- idealism,
- artistic interests, and
- attraction to the unusual, the complex and the mysterious.

Torrance (1980) later provided an additional list of common characteristics, which may help parents and teachers to recognise the creative child who

- is full of ideas and sees the relationship between them;
- is imaginative and enjoys pretending;
- has flexibility of ideas and thoughts;
- constructs, builds and then re-builds;
- can cope with several ideas at once;
- is always telling others about their discoveries or inventions;
- likes to do things differently from the norm.

However, Torrance also lists characteristics that may be negative and, therefore, irritate parents and teachers. These include:

- stubbornness;
- uncooperativeness;

- non-participation in certain activities;
- low interest in details and indifference to some common conventions and courtesies;
- disorganised and sloppy about matters which appear unimportant;
- temperamental, demanding and emotional.

Both these lists indicate the diversity of creative abilities, as well as the difficulty of relying on a checklist only (see Chapter 3).

Because of the numerous areas in which a student can be gifted and talented, it is not surprising that there are probably as many different strategies and policies for identifying these children as there are definitions. If we accept that gifted children are those who excel consistently or show the potential to excel consistently in one or more areas of human endeavour to the extent that they need and could benefit from specially planned educational services beyond those normally provided by the standard school programme, a broad definition should consider the following talent areas:

- general intellectual ability;
- specific academic aptitude (an aptitude in a specific subject area);
- creative and productive thinking (divergent thinking that results in unconventional responses to conventional tasks);
- leadership and social awareness ability (assumes leadership roles, but also is accepted by others as a leader);
- visual and performing arts ability (graphic arts, sculpture, music or dance);
- pyschomotor ability (mechanical skills or athletic ability).

Each child is unique, however, and any attempt to define these children will be a generalisation. It is impossible to cover every individual variation of ability and talent, which is what makes this work so fascinating. None the less, defining gifts and talents is important because the particular definition will determine the selection of children for special provision. Gifted children who are poor, disabled, underachieving, female or from ethnic minority groups, may be discriminated against.

## CASE STUDIES OF FOUR VERY DIFFERENT CHILDREN

Case studies of gifted and talented children can help us recognise many of the characteristics of these children and identify their needs. After each subject summary, there are questions for discussion and some suggestions for helping the child. These cases are recommended for in-service workshops or simply to help readers focus on these children.

The first three case studies may give the false impression that all gifted children have problems. Hitchfield's (1973) and Freeman's (1991) research gave us no evidence to suggest that these children had more problems than any other group. Most gifted children do consistently well and are happy, well-balanced people. Some schools have a large share of gifted children, 98 per cent of whom take A levels and go into higher education, and few of whom have problems. The fourth case study represents a positive success where both parents and school cope well to make an able child happy and high-achieving in most areas of the curriculum.

### Paul, aged 5½

*Background information*

Paul is the second of two children. His older sister, Sarah (aged 7), is a quiet girl, who is doing well, but not outstandingly, in school, and who is undemanding and rather undemonstrative at home. Paul, by contrast, is very prominent. At home he takes up a great deal of his parents' time and energy. He is boundlessly energetic, sleeps only six hours a night, is exhaustingly interested in everything around him, and spends hours dismantling everything mechanical or electrical. He had to be withdrawn from playgroup because staff were unable to manage his behaviour with other children. He has few friends in the neighbourhood and his parents feel 'criticised' about their management of their child.

He was admitted to school early at his parents' request. He already reads fluently, with the accuracy and understanding of a much older child. However he dislikes the process of writing, declaring it to be 'boring', and will write only under duress. His ability to work with numbers is quite advanced. He can add and subtract with numbers up to 100, and enjoys working on number problems in his head. He has periods when he will concentrate intensely, almost obsessively, on a task which captures his interest, but for the most part he moves about restlessly, visiting other groups to see what they are doing, making comments and suggestions to them (usually resented), or actively interfering or disrupting their play. He has become unpopular with both children and staff, and is becoming quite a problem. Paul shows considerable ability but his behaviour is destructive and he is rejected by other children.

*Points for discussion*

School

(1) What would you see as being Paul's educational and social needs?

(2) How might these be met within the school?

Parent

(1) What would you see as being Paul's needs – from school?

(2) What does Paul need from you and the family?

(3) How might you assist the school?

(4) What other forms of support would you welcome?

*Some suggestions to help Paul*

Paul is perhaps in the wrong school. He is a bright boy who needs a very skilful teacher who could harness his energies and interference with other children and get them on his side.

Educational needs

- Discovering an interest in writing/presentation (using a computer, tape recorder, visual materials, word processor) – he must find it worthwhile getting his work on view.
- Learning to stick with a task (setting criteria for completing a task and insisting it gets done to those criteria); if he were older he could be given a contract (see p.94).
- Accepting time limits for teacher attention and non-interference of others – a clock which he can watch to see when he can change tasks or visit other areas could be motivating.
- Being given interesting and stimulating problems (such as in maths) which tax his ingenuity, instead of routine computations.
- Constructive use of his reading abilities – opportunities to do something for others with these abilities.

Social needs

- Accepting class rules and expectations.
- Learning to take part in group activities.
- Coping with frustration (teacher patience, with acknowledgement to Paul that they understand why he's angry).
- Plenty of variety in activities, with gradual extension of the time he spends on them (some physical activities before bed might help him sleep!).
- Tolerance from teachers.
- Sense of humour from teachers.
- Sharing (of ideas, help, time) with other teachers – Paul could spend some time with other teachers, or with his head teacher.
- Finding what he likes to do most and using this as a reward.
- Advice and support from parents – it would be interesting to check Paul's diet because some foods and food additives can cause hyperactivity.
- Advice, support and programme planning from the school educational psychologist.

- Suitable materials to meet his interest in things mechanical and in dismantling.
- Six hours sleep is no problem – give him access to a light, his toys and books and explain to him what the needs of others are – more sleep, private time, etc.

### Elizabeth, aged 10+

*Background information*

Elizabeth is an only child. Her parents were in their late thirties when she was born. Elizabeth was precocious as an infant, learning to read when she was two, and showing an unusual talent in a number of fields. By the age of five she was reading books usually thought suitable for twelve year olds, she had started learning the piano and the guitar, and she was taking dancing lessons. At twelve she is still an excellent all-round achiever: she plays the piano, the clarinet and the guitar, she is a member of the local gymnastics team, and she produces a consistently high level of work in school.

However, Elizabeth is not terribly popular in school. Her achievements and abilities are recognised but no one feels very comfortable with her. She is a rather tense and brittle person, and tends to make teachers and pupils feel rather second-rate and inadequate. She does not suffer fools gladly and is quick to put people right. Because of this, teachers may want to 'put her down'. Although she produces high-quality work, she reacts very badly to adverse comments, and shows great distress when anything but praise is given to her work. Nothing less than consistent A grades satisfies her.

Elizabeth's parents provide a poor social role model. They do not mix easily and appear to be a very self-contained couple. They are enormously proud of their daughter's success, and devote much, if not most, of their time to supporting her in her activities. This over-dependency is compounded by Elizabeth's own over-dependency on a need to achieve in order to get pleasure from herself and her work.

Despite her apparent successes, Elizabeth does not seem to enjoy life as much as she might. She appears to have been mismanaged at school, with no negotiation of her role, and to have very low self-esteem.

*Points for discussion*

School

(1) What do you see as the major concerns in working with Elizabeth?
(2) What do you think needs to be done to help Elizabeth continue to achieve at an appropriate level for her abilities, but which would help her out of

the stress of striving all the time for top grades?
(3)  What could teachers do to help Elizabeth feel more at ease in her relationships, and less destructively demanding of herself and others?
(4)  What are the danger areas in the future for this child?
(5)  What would you want to be talking about with her parents? What help might you want from them?
(6)  How might you work with the parents?

*Some suggestions to help Elizabeth*

Positively encouraging Elizabeth's academic achievements might increase her arrogant behaviour and further distance her from her peers socially. It is vital to introduce safe areas in which she can face difficulties, without producing a negative response. A change of school, where she could be counselled and given a fresh start, would be a last resort.

• Set Elizabeth tasks for which there are no assessment outcomes.
• Set her tasks which call for collaboration and cooperation with others. Joining in team games and the school orchestra would be helpful.
• Set her open-ended tasks and problems which offer a range of outcomes.
• Present her with tasks beyond her present capacity, with a planned strategy for helping her face her feelings when she is not able to produce 'right' answers.
• Provide opportunities for Elizabeth to take part in activities away from home.
• Help her respond more positively to criticism or comment.
• Set up joint planning on open-ended creative activities to take place out of school.
• Offer the parents counselling as well, because they appear to be trotting behind Elizabeth and not alongside her.
• Give Elizabeth friendly common sense advice – she has the ability to understand sound explanations. Children can be quite shocked when confronted with the consequences of their behaviour in a friendly context and not the usual disciplinary one.

## Adolescent: Martin, aged 14

*Background information*

Martin is considered to be a 'walking disaster' by his teachers. He seems to live in a world of his own. He is never where he should be, and he is invariably late for classes. He had great difficulties with the early stages of reading and writing, and never mastered the intricacies of spelling. His handwriting is appalling, and he is reluctant to put pen to paper. He has a very sharp wit and has become the class clown.

He was quite interested in secondary school in the first two years, when he enjoyed the wide range of subjects. Last year things began to go wrong for him. He found teachers to be more concerned with maintaining their authority than with the pursuit of truth. He found the move to set syllabuses very frustrating because there were fewer opportunities for 'theorising' and 'playing' with ideas.

His relationships with most teachers are extremely poor, since he tends to challenge and question both their authority and their knowledge. He is also rather dismissive of the views of many of his peers. His science teachers, however, value his contribution to class discussion, since he shows remarkable insight and understanding, beyond that of most young people of his age. He would like to devote himself exclusively to science, and science-related subjects, and dispense with the rest. He should be capable of achieving good examination results, were his present attitude and ability to present his work to change.

Martin is in a difficult phase at home. He is argumentative and restless. He is hopelessly untidy, and often unkind to his young sister. He is angry at his parents' accusations that he is lazy, and claims that when he is spending long periods watching TV he is in fact working hard in his head.

One is tempted to ask what Martin gets out of life in school!

*Points for discussion*

(1) What are the main issues for the school in helping Martin through the current phase?
(2) What could the school do to ease the present difficulties?
(3) What might individual teachers do to improve their relationships with Martin?
(4) What help might the school want from elsewhere, and how might such help be woven into what goes on in the school?
(5) What help does the school want from the parents?
(6) What help could the school offer to the parents?

*Some suggestions to help Martin*

Martin is a good illustration that his problems are nothing to do with his ability. He is just an unlucky adolescent in personal and emotional trouble. The drop in standards is a worrying sign. The main issue is to get Martin to believe he is being taken seriously, that the school recognises his difficulties and dilemmas, acknowledges his abilities and welcomes them, and wants to find a positive solution.

• Provide opportunities for Martin to express his ideas in class without damaging the other pupils' and the teacher's morale.

- Persuade him to accept some help with work presentation without damaging his ego; drama activities would probably help.
- Help him become more self-organised, which he is willing to work on.
- Get a negotiated agreement with him on his behaviour and his commitment to work.
- Find a 'personal' tutor with whom he would meet regularly to set up action plans on different aspects of his work and behaviour, with regular reviews.
- Have a case conference with Martin and his teachers to agree on approaches to assessing his work, on a policy for presentation criteria and on a policy and process for him to negotiate decisions on homework and assignments. Are there responsibilities in school to which he would contribute?
- Discuss honestly with him the dilemma in which he places his teachers. Get some agreement or a contract on how he will manage classroom discussion, and how teachers will show him respect too. Ask him how he wants his work assessed and to provide commentary for his own work. Get him to set his own targets.
- Consultations with a psychologist might help in discussions about how to get away from being the class clown and how to become more organised.
- Arrange contacts with other local resources or college interest groups for enrichment possibilities.
- Have regular discussions with his parents to present a joint approach.
- Identify areas where parental support/supervision could be helpful without damaging Martin's self-esteem.
- Establish a non-judgmental, supportive dialogue and take a confident, positive stance towards Martin.

## Frances, aged 6

Frances is the elder of our two children. Her younger brother, Joseph, is $3\frac{1}{2}$ years old. As a baby she slept little by day, but settled down fairly well at night. Frances has always been demanding of our time, in the sense that she has always insisted on participating in every activity however unsuitable for a baby or toddler! Additionally she showed very little interest in the company of other children until she started school, and preferred the company of adults.

Even as a baby Frances was fascinated by books and language and seemed to possess a 'drive' to read. She achieved this around $2\frac{1}{2}$–3 years, and still reads voraciously. Frances has now settled happily at school. After a year in the reception class she jumped an academic year and then began to mix more easily with other children, although at times she still prefers her own company. Today Frances gets enormous pleasure from playing chess, singing in the choir and learning the recorder, all activities she has taken up this year at school.

At home Frances can still be restless and excitable but will settle down with single-minded determination if something captures her interest, or an adult will play chess with her or present her with a page of sums to complete!

Frances has always been an affectionate child, although fairly volatile when crossed. She loathes being in the wrong, and can get very upset when things are not going smoothly. Fortunately her brother has a more phlegmatic approach to life and they get on well together.

Our main concern is that we feel she is frustrated by the slow pace of some lessons at school and we feel she is underachieving. She seems to do so much of the same especially in mathematics.

# CHAPTER 3

# Identification

An instrument has been developed in advance of the needs of its possessor.
(Alfred Wallace)

It is the only example of evolution providing a species with an organ which it does
not know how to use; a luxury organ, which will take its owner thousands of years
to learn to put to proper use – if it ever does!                              (Arthur Koestler)

The discussion of talented and gifted children is fundamentally linked with the
need to develop identification techniques and procedures which a busy teacher
can use in the classroom. Because we now accept that children can be gifted or
talented in various areas, it is not surprising that many sources of information
are typically used to identify such children. However, these sources can be
categorised into three major areas: teacher appraisal of their children, the use of
rating scales and checklists, and the administration of different types of
standardised tests.

## TEACHER APPRAISAL OF CHILDREN

Obviously, good professional teachers should know their children. They play
the most important part in the identification of gifted and talented students. As
a first step, the head teacher and the staff of the school should ask themselves
the following simple questions: do we have the best possible system for
assessing, recording and communicating the needs of each child accurately,
and are these records accessible to teachers and passed on from year to year?
The National Curriculum and its assessment methodology should help
considerably in this respect. A system needs to be established for the clear
recording of pupils' achievements and progress.

   In the secondary stage of education, where more than one teacher is
responsible for recording progress, the system should include procedures for
collating all the information about a child into one record. There should also
be a procedure for regular and frequent exchange of information between the
teachers contributing to the total record. On p.35 readers will find a suggested
Referral Form for gifted, talented or underachieving children and a method for
recording observations. It is essential that exceptional performance in any one
subject should be known to teachers of other subjects so that disparities and
underachievement may be considered. Ogilvie (1973) suggests that a teacher's
subjective assessment of a pupil can be inaccurate if there is a tendency to rate

most highly those pupils who are persevering, conforming, tidy and industrious. Many gifted pupils are careless, untidy and reluctant to write, since their speed of thinking is faster than their recording skills. It is, therefore, quite easy to mark a child down because of the poor quality of writing produced: teachers need to take time to look at the underlying vocabulary and knowledge. This process of identification consists of making assessments and judgements. It must perforce contain a subjective and an objective element. Any form of identification can be seen to lie on a continuum between these two areas.

There are certain broad principles which a teacher should consider when trying to identify talented and gifted children:

(1) ensure that the process of identification is rooted in areas that the child is being allowed to experience;

(2) ensure that the child can express her- or himself and listen carefully; and

(3) ensure that the process of identification points towards useful developments and extension of the child's work.

Although teachers are extremely busy, with a multiplicity of jobs to fulfil, a professional teacher will try to screen the children. This relies heavily on teacher referral. It is obviously easier to do this in the primary sector, where teachers will probably teach a whole class for a whole year, than in the secondary phase, where a specialist teacher may teach perhaps 300 different children in one week and it is extremely difficult to know the children well. Contrary to this, Coleman (1985) found that teachers had more difficulty identifying younger children than older secondary-level children. In addition, Howley et al. (1986) found that the more mixed the ethnic and racial composition of the class, the more difficult it was for a teacher to identify giftedness. Denton and Postlethwaite (1985) undertook an interesting piece of research in a number of comprehensive schools in Oxfordshire on the effectiveness of testing secondary children in four subject areas and compared this with teacher-based identification. Teachers were more effective at identifying children in mathematics and English than in physics and French (see Table 3.1). It is interesting that the school that had the closest match in English was also the school that had the worst match in physics. This may reflect the difference between teacher-based and test-based judgement and may be due to teacher variation rather than to the impact of different school size, type or organisation.

**Table 3.1:** Overall percentage of test-identified pupils also identified by teacher. Number of pupils in brackets.

| School | English | French | Physics | Maths |
|---|---|---|---|---|
| All schools | 61 (213) | 51 (210) | 45 (216) | 61 (215) |
| Range of % | 33–75 | 25–73 | 17–75 | 36–78 |

It is interesting to compare these figures with the results obtained by Pegnato and Birch (1959). They asked teachers to nominate children who were 'mentally gifted' and matched these nominations against those who scored 136 or more on an individually administered Stanford-Binet IQ test. They found that teachers identified only 45 per cent of those with high IQs, and also that approximately 31 per cent of those identified as gifted by the teachers had average IQs. We should note, however, that there were some limitations in this research in that IQ was the only criterion used by the researchers to determine giftedness, whereas the teachers applied seven criteria, including teacher appraisal. Both Denton and Postlethwaite (1985) and Gear (1978) stated that in-service training could help teachers assess such children. Gear noted that trained teachers correctly identified approximately 86 per cent, whereas the untrained correctly identified only 40 per cent. It was shown that the trained teachers helped eliminate some of the ambiguity about the nature of giftedness.

Teachers should also provide a systematic record of their observation of pupils' current behaviour, aptitudes and interests. Observation recording of skills does not come naturally. It would, therefore, be helpful to have a structured framework within which such observations can be formulated.

It is also essential that teachers provide a creative learning environment in which children have the opportunity to show their gifts and talents. By a creative learning environment, I mean a classroom in which thinking is valued far more than memory and in which the child's contribution is valued and respected. It is also a classroom where the teacher supports and reinforces children's unusual ideas, where failure is seen as an opportunity to help students realise errors and meet acceptable standards, and where the classroom procedures are adapted to the students' interests and ideas wherever possible. This involves a delicate balance between psychological safety and freedom, so that pupils are prepared to take risks, and a balance between the freedom to think and to be adventurous and the behavioural freedom which leads to chaos. Teachers in such classrooms encourage divergent learning activities as well as listening and laughing with the students. The teacher is the facilitator, the resource manager, the enthusiast, the guide, the prompter, the change agent. The teacher provides a warm, supportive atmosphere and allows children to make choices and to be a part of the decision-making process. Such a teacher is not the only authority with the one right answer, because no one can possibly know all there is to know about any one subject. It is unfortunate that there are still a great number of non-creative classrooms where there is little freedom to explore, and the teacher is authoritarian, rigid, obsessed with keeping order, unwilling to give individuals time, and insensitive to pupils' emotional needs.

There is a close relationship between the concept of giftedness, the characteristics of gifted and talented children, their identification and programmes of learning for them. Identification should be viewed as a part of good teaching, a continuous process that anticipates further challenging learning experiences with a quality end product. Identification is then an evaluation process that teachers undertake in the classroom, rather than a series of tests administered by outside specialists. (This is not to deny that checklists and standardised achievement tests have their place.)

I am indebted to Dr Don McAlpine for a copy of his excellent lecture to NZAGC in 1991, in which he states:

> The so-called 'responsive environment' approach to the identification of these children contains many advantages. First of all, it offers more professional responsibility to teachers to assess children's abilities. Secondly, teachers become more interested in the programme if they are also involved in the identification. Thirdly, identification is embedded naturally into the day to day learning and teaching activities of the regular classroom. The general quality of teaching for all children is thereby improved. The gifted programme is not an oasis in a desert, but the whole classroom is an oasis. Fourthly, identification becomes closely linked to objectives of the programme. Identification should always be seen as a means to an end and never as an end in itself.

What are some of the limitations of the responsive environment approach? The quality of teachers is very uneven in respect to methods of identification. There are, therefore, threats to the reliability and validity of the identification process. As a result, some children may be overlooked while others, for example teacher-pleasers, may be included. In large classes in mainstream schools, identification is yet another task to perform, with a consequent increase in workload and commitment to the programme which must follow. Finally, teachers with indifferent or negative attitudes to gifted and talented children may do nothing at all to identify or cater for such children.

### Exercise: myths and misconceptions

(1) Read through the following lists and check which items are misconceptions.

(2) Tick which three you agree with the most and star those you disagree with and consider to be myths.

(3)  Think of the most gifted and talented child you know and circle which items apply to that particular individual.

I am indebted to Richard Lange and Mark German for giving me permission to use the following list.

*Characteristics of gifted learners*

Gifted children:

- have everything going their way
- are more emotionally stable and mature than their non-gifted peers
- prefer to work alone
- are model students
- always reveal their giftedness
- are organised and neat
- are well rounded
- are creative
- are good learners
- are very verbal
- have good handwriting
- are good spellers
- have very supportive parents and come from good homes
- have a low tolerance for slower students
- are perfectionists
- work harder than average kids
- look or act differently

*Identification procedures*

- gifted students always reveal their intelligence
- gifted students are respected and looked up to by their peers
- Asians tend to have the highest percentage of gifted students
- gifted handicapped students are best served within the special education environment
- highly gifted children become socially maladjusted
- gifted children can no more be stopped from achieving their potential than a cannonball can be diverted from its path once it has been fired
- girls appear with much greater frequency than boys do in gifted programmes
- culturally diverse gifted students have great difficulty fitting into traditional programmes for the gifted
- non-identified siblings feel left out

Identification procedures should include these items:

- IQ testing
- test scores achievement
- parent inventory
- self-inventory
- staff inventory/checklist
- student grades/report cards
- student products
- subjective teacher comments

*Programme models and delivery systems*

- gifted students need constant challenges
- teachers prefer to work with gifted students
- double promotion can be harmful to gifted students
- gifted programmes should be a reward to gifted students
- teachers of gifted students should be gifted themselves
- gifted classes end up with the best teachers
- gifted students learn things with only one presentation
- total segregation is the best model
- pull-out programmes cause double-duty
- mentorship programmes are not worth the effort it takes to organise them.

## A GENERAL IDENTIFICATION CHECKLIST

Checklists have been developed to improve the efficiency of teacher judgement. However, they are rather subjective and often poorly constructed, and give no indication how well a child must score to be considered gifted.

They are not tests to determine whether or not a particular child is exceptionally able. Each child is unique, and any one child may or may not show some, all or none of the characteristics described. However, checklists can prove helpful in alerting parents and teachers to the possibility that they may be misjudging some of their children and it would encourage them to look for signs or talents which they might have so far failed to acknowledge. They can influence strategies and can open up a dialogue with children and parents.

Many different checklists have been put forward – some fairly short and concise, others of great length and all-embracing detail. More recently, specific checklists have been devised for subject specialists at the secondary stage. The completed checklist in Figure 3.1 attempts to include the most commonly mentioned features, without becoming unnecessarily complex. The results are typical in that the child is bored with routine work whereas other characteristics are clustered towards the exceptional end.

| Child's Name: *Jane Smith* | | Sex: *F* Date of Birth 03.04.81 | | Age: *9y 3m* | |
|---|---|---|---|---|---|
| Characteristics | Poor | Weak | Average | Good | Exceptional |
| Use of language | | | | | x |
| Reasoning ability | | | | | x |
| Speed of thought | | | | | x |
| Imagination | | | | x | |
| Memory | | | | | x |
| Observation | | | | x | |
| Concentration | | | x | | |
| Whether questioning | | | | | x |
| Makes original suggestions | | | | x | |
| Problem solving | | | | | x |
| Extent of reading | | | | | x |
| Routine work | x | | | | |

**Figure 3.1:** A completed teacher's checklist showing the ability profile of a possibly gifted pupil

None of the behaviours listed should be taken as proof of high ability but they can alert teachers and parents to the need to question the reasons for their occurrence. If a child scores highly on quite a number of these characteristics, then you should enquire further into a child's abilities.

The rest of this chapter will look at a variety of methods for identifying gifted and talented children in the major talent areas. Some children show themselves as very able by their high energy or intense curiosity, others are more difficult to spot and deliberately hide their talents. A multi-dimensional, integrated approach is therefore necessary. More emphasis is put on areas where there has been less research, recognition and application in the classroom. I start with a question, action and purpose exercise (see p.36).

## INTELLIGENCE AND ITS ASSESSMENT

> Intelligence can only come when there is freedom – freedom to think, to observe, to question.
>
> (Krishnamurti)

One of the most controversial and yet fascinating aspects of education is intelligence. Intelligence has been defined as the ability to see relationships and to use this ability to solve problems. Some psychologists facetiously define intelligence as the ability to do intelligence tests! A problem of definition has

# Identification procedure

Initial concern from parents, teacher or pupil that a pupil may be exceptionally able or talented and that their curriculum needs may not be being fully met.

| Question | Action | Purpose |
|---|---|---|
| What information do we have to make us believe this child has exceptional ability or talent? | Summarise all available information<br>– educational history<br>– parental<br>– medical<br>Analyse reason for concern<br>– peer/teacher view. | To identify past observation or advantages to learning.<br>To identify patterns of performance.<br>To clarify intuitive responses. |
| Is our intuition borne out in performance? | Objective teacher observation based on an agreed structured framework. | To provide a systematic record of current behaviour interests and aptitudes. Is performance affected by different situations? |
| What do our observations indicate? How should we proceed? | Compare with a checklist of behavioural criteria (gifted and under-achieving). | – to devise an individual profile<br>– to identify possible underachievement. |
| Have we enough information? (What else do we need to know and why? – see criteria for using test) | Select a standardised test – using criteria. | To suplement the existing information and inform the planned action and curriculum provision. |
| What do we do with this information? | Systematically and succintly record the information. | – for future reference<br>– so there is a reference for future action planning<br>– to give a rationale for future action planning? |
| How do we meet the needs of this pupil? | – inform all involved (teachers/parents/pupils).<br>– agree criteria for future performance.<br>– plan future action.<br>– agree a time to review. | Common awareness. To provide curriculum planning. |

Request outside help at any point in this process but such requests should outline at what point on the continuum help is requested and why.

burdened psychologists since Cicero coined the word 'intelligentia' based on ideas used by both Aristotle and Plato.

All children's formal work in school can be influenced by the outcome of intelligence testing. In addition, high or low intelligence can carry important vocational and social significance for our children. In many countries the bottom-line instrument for confirming suspected high ability is an individual intelligence test.

The other area of controversy is the continuing debate over whether intelligence is inherited or determined by environmental factors. I find it impossible to conceive that intellectual superiority can be attributed to any one factor, whether it is environmental, genetic or neurological. Clark (1988) maintains that gifted children have different neurological and biochemical makeup and Sternberg (1985) equally convincingly argues that intelligence is determined by the amount, type and degree of environmental stimulation that a child receives, including the quality of the environment and the attitudes of parents.

Academic ability is probably the major reason for gifted children being identified initially, because such children perform well in academic subjects. They are also persistent, respond well to instruction and have good study skills. These children often do well in intelligence tests because they process information quickly, have better memories, have greater accuracy and are good at abstract thinking.

Not all gifted children have these attributes, however. Some have difficulty in mastering basic skills. This is why this book emphasises a multi-dimensional approach to identification and support. It is little wonder, therefore, that both parents and teachers take a great deal of interest in intelligence, but at the same time that there are many misconceptions about its measurement and significance which can affect a child's progress.

The most common tests of intelligence used by educational psychologists in the UK are the Wechsler Intelligence Scale for Children (WISC-R UK) and the British Ability Scale (BAS). These tests comprise a range of separate subtests from which an Intelligence Quotient (IQ) can be calculated. When David Wechsler put together the subtests of the WISC he identified those that were felt to measure some of the underlying abilities related to school achievement. His choice of subtest was to some extent arbitrary, but the statistical data available in the WISC Manual indicate that the subtests correlate between 0.3 and 0.5, which is modest but acceptable. However, it has been observed that a number of tests, for example tests of mechanical ability, were found not to correlate with the other items of the WISC and were therefore rejected. For practitioners who would value information about the whole range of a child's abilities this somewhat ruthless selection of subtests is unfortunate, though the core subtests available provide a reasonable range with which to obtain a profile of a child's skills. The BAS, designed by Colin Elliot and others, contains a much wider selection of subtests and therefore can enable the psychologist to build up a more accurate profile of skills and abilities for some age groups. These tests, unlike the earlier IQ tests, which comprised predominantly objective items requiring one right answer, have a higher subjective content with more sophisticated methods of interpretation. These provide the best consensus test to date, but there is still much to be learnt regarding what tests really test in the light of the ever-changing theory of intelligence.

These tests include two major types: group attainment tests, which can be useful indicators of ability; and individual tests, open to teachers, which are designed to reveal levels of cognitive ability and potential. These tests require considerable time and expertise to administer and, therefore, should be undertaken by an educational psychologist. Such tests may be administered shortly after pupils enter a school or college, or when there is concern at underachievement. However, there is a need for staff to be aware of the purposes for which the tests are to be used, to know how to interpret the results and to recognise the limitations of such tests. Additionally, there is a need to counter the probability of early categorisation and labelling of pupils and self-fulfilling prophecies. Some aspects and forms of high ability do not lend themselves to standardised testing, which additionally limits the value of such tests. In doubtful cases, schools should contact their educational psychologist, who will be able to offer more detailed and accurate assessment and advice. Although an intelligence test may have been designed under the misapprehension that intelligence is a unitary concept, this does not preclude its use in a more flexible way to build up a cognitive profile. It is only to be expected that the mean scores that children obtain on intelligence test subscales increase as the child's age increases.

'Viewing mind' from an entirely different perspective, Sternberg and Davidson (1986) considered the development of children with markedly greater intellectual achievements than is common. They identified three factors in the genesis of giftedness: 'intelligence, creativity and commitment'. They felt that gifted children might be expected to score well on broadly based intelligence tests such as the WISC and that a high score on the WISC was in some way a prerequisite for high levels of achievement, but by no means a sufficient feature. Creativity was included as one of the three factors because they felt that, in order to be able to think originally or to see or understand things that others do not, a child would need to challenge prevailing conceptual frameworks and, as it were, stand outside the conventional ways of looking at things.

There appear to be children who have an aptitude for creativity as apart from academic aptitude. Indeed, there is no correlation between the two after a threshold IQ of 100 (Ogilvie, 1973). Such children are often referred to as being divergent thinkers and educationalists frequently use the Guilford model of fluency, originality, flexibility and foresight, as opposed to convergent thinking, which emphasises the more traditional academic skills of memory, classification and reasoning ability. Some distinctions can be seen in Table 3.2, where the IQ questions have only one correct answer whereas the creativity questions stress the importance of many answers. Creativity is discussed in more detail later.

**Table 3.2:** The difference between IQ test questions and creativity test questions

| Typical IQ test questions | Typical; creativity test question |
|---|---|
| 1. Glove is to hand as shoe is to . . . | What would happen if everyone was born with three fingers and no thumb |
| 2. What is a bucket? | How many uses can you think of for a bucket? |
| 3. If a girl goes into a shop and buys 37p of sweets and gives the man 50p, how much change will she get back? | How many different ways can you think of to get an answer of 7? |

The dispute concerning the relative independence of intelligence and creativity continues. Intelligence of over IQ 100 may be the best predictor of academic achievement, but above this point increases in creativity become more significant for the prediction of achievement of some children. This is generally seen to be a feature of creativity, though by no means a sufficient characteristic.

Sternberg and Davidson's third factor, 'commitment', was considered to be very significant because they felt that it is only with great motivation and, indeed, dedication and sacrifice that the creative gifts of adults become apparent and that it is only with strong motivation that children are able to achieve in school or in an academic situation. Renzulli (1977) also included commitment as an essential factor in gifted achievement. This factor helps us to make sense of intelligence and cognitive profiles.

A consistent feature of much of our understanding of intelligence is that those human characteristics that in Western growth-oriented economies confer personal and social advantages are the characteristics most closely associated with the notion of intelligence. People who can manage a company efficiently or succeed in their chosen profession are invariably thought of by others as intelligent. It may be, therefore, that our understanding of the mix of skills and abilities that constitute intelligence is a feature of the social objectives and values that we share in Western society. In other societies, the mix of abilities that enable a person to find water in the most severe desert conditions or to make an accurate blowpipe could equally well be regarded as a hallmark of an intelligent person. It is possible, using modern psychometric measures, to identify the cognitive profiles that are associated with success in different professions and in different cultures, without necessarily putting a value judgement on those profiles and declaring that one is somehow better than another. Unfortunately, the present generation of psychometric tests does not enable the psychologist to build up more than a rough and ready profile on which broader decisions might be made.

The current difficulties with profiling would appear to reside in the limitations of the subtests that comprise the separate batteries. Subtests have to be easy to administer and should not take too long to complete, otherwise there would be a risk of maladministration of the test and of anyone taking it becoming fatigued, thus causing an invalid estimate of test performance. The standardisation of tests is a long and expensive procedure. It takes many years to prepare a reliable measure. The material of the tests rapidly becomes dated so test producers are hard pressed to maintain the validity of the tests they have already published, let alone develop new ones. The availability of broad measures of intelligence, such as the WISC and the BAS, is thus limited, and in many cases research has been carried out using simple paper and pencil tests. These typically involve identifying which of a collection of items is not part of the group, completing a sequence or constructing a word from a pattern or a sequence of letters. Although there is a correlation between the results of these tests and the aggregate scores of the broad-range measures of intelligence, unlike the broad-range tests they do not yield a cognitive profile. As we have seen, an isolated IQ score cannot of itself offer much information since the meaning of the tests resides in the profile constructed from the results.

## SCHOOL ACHIEVEMENT AND GIFTEDNESS

If a child has the right balance of abilities to achieve well in an academic setting, what significance does this have for the child? A distinction has often been made between high-achieving children in a school situation, referred to as 'schoolhouse gifted' by Renzulli (1977), and creativity in adults in the fields of, say, mathematics, engineering or the arts. It has been proposed that the abilities necessary for higher school achievement, often in the form of nine GCSEs at Grade A, are quite different from the ability needed to make a significant contribution to research or an outstanding achievement in the arts. Attention has been drawn to the differing conditions in which 'schoolhouse giftedness' and creative adult achievement take place. School achievement is the result of hard work in a wide range of differing areas of the curriculum where the level of study is fairly superficial and the problems that need to be solved are normally quite clearly defined. Adult creative achievement, on the other hand, is usually the result of single-minded dedication, often extending over many years, to the resolution of problems that are usually vague and quite undefined.

For example, in order to be able to solve some mathematical problems, it was necessary to invent specific mathematical techniques for doing so. The incentive was the need to solve a physical or mathematical problem, but the invention of the technique itself – for example, calculus, complex numbers, non-Euclidian geometry – was a purely creative act. It should not come as any surprise to find that many adults who have a proven record of creative academic achievement do not score especially well on paper and pencil measures of intelligence. Indeed, intelligence tests are based on tasks with clearly defined problems and answers that are either right or wrong. No satisfactory test has yet been devised that can measure a person's ability to resolve ill-defined problems with no clearly correct or incorrect solutions. There have been attempts, however. Getzels and Jackson (1962) devised specific tests of the form, 'How many uses can you think of for a box of chocolates, a dead cat, a sleeping child'. This style of assessment is included in the current BAS as a subtest, but these tests can be scored only by totting up the number of distinct uses identified: little regard can be given to the quality of the responses. It is a matter of personal opinion, at the present time, whether these tests really reflect a relevant dimension of creativity.

## THE EDUCATIONAL IMPLICATIONS OF TESTS AND COGNITIVE PROFILES

The application of intelligence testing to everyday classroom practice has been more successful in the area of identifying children's strengths and cognitive weaknesses. Educational programmes can be designed to match the cognitive profile of a child in such a way that areas of success can be guaranteed where there are known strengths and programmes can be very carefully constructed in areas in which the child is weak to ensure that there is success here too. Testing has been used for some time to identify underachievement, but again the profiling approach can help teachers to be more specific about the areas in which underachievement is likely and can alert them to the specific needs of children in those areas. Underlying much of the interpretation of test results have been information-processing models of mental structure. It should be possible, by carefully considering the components of educational tasks such as reading, to match aspects of the task to a child's cognitive profile and thereby explain high achievement or specific difficulty. It is now possible to design educational programmes that take into account the evident weaknesses of children in specific skill areas. Information-processing models focus on the role of short-term as opposed to long-term memory, the encoding and decoding of linguistic information, as well as the broader aspects of flexibility of concept formation and inspection times. At the present stage of our knowledge, however, an interpretation of cognitive profiles and an appreciation of the associated educational difficulties cannot be simply deduced but relies on long-standing educational and clinical experience. By themselves the test results are of only limited value. Moreover, tests take very little account of attention skill deficits, and observations about these cannot easily be integrated into assessment findings. Thus, the assessment of intelligence appears to be in part scientific and in part intuitive.

## Creativity

Creativity is now firmly established as one of the significant categories associated with giftedness and talent. The widening of the concept of giftedness to include creativity and other abilities, has made it a multi-category concept. However, we should remind ourselves that this has not always been so. In early studies of the gifted, intelligence, rather narrowly defined, was the sole criterion. Too little emphasis is placed on the development of creativity in all gifted students and even less significance is placed on identifying creatively gifted students. Those who hold on to the narrow definition will leave significant numbers of creatively gifted students out of programmes for the gifted and talented. In addition, we should remember that some of the greatest strengths of disadvantaged and culturally different students are their creative skills and motivations.

At a time when charges of elitism are often aimed at programmes for the gifted, and the very word 'gifted' arouses antagonism in some communities, parents and educators could do far worse than to consider the positive and beneficial impact that programmes centred on creativity and the development of creative talent might have in their respective communities.

One of the problems which surfaces when we explore the role of creativity in the gifted population involves identification. Nearly everyone recognises or knows what creativity is, in general, but there is less agreement on precise definitions and identification instruments. The term has multiple meanings and can be defined quite differently by different people (Klein, 1982). I suspect that most of us in education use the word every day without considering its real meaning.

Urban (1988) states that high creativity is the ability to create a new, unusual and surprising product by perceiving, processing and utilising a maximum of available information; by associating and combining this information with data from experience or imagined elements and data; by synthesising all parts or elements into a theme or holistic Gestalt in whatever shape or form; and, lastly, by communicating and sharing the creative product with others. McAlpine (1988) asserts that consideration of creativity as the resolution of conflict and the fusion of thinking, feeling, sensing and intuition helps our understanding of creative thinking. Wallace (1986) too states that creativity is a resolution of conflict and reminds us that Jung saw creativity as 'the balance between the conscious and the sub-conscious, the rational and the irrational, extroversion and introversion, divergent and convergent'. Vaughan (1977) also sees creativity as a delicate balancing of opposites which produces a new integration or synthesis. A creative process can be maintained only by holding the opposites in a state of dynamic tension.

Clark (1988) has elaborated an integrated model of creativity consisting of four major dimensions: (i) thinking; (ii) feeling; (iii) intuition; (iv) sensing. The thinking aspect involves sensing and solving problems and the use of divergent thinking abilities. Children make sense of their world by using their senses and primary school teachers use this aspect admirably. The feeling aspect focuses on emotional well-being and self-actualising – if you think well of yourself you can meet your creative potential. The intuitive component employs imagery, fantasy and impulses to assist breakthroughs to the pre-conscious and unconscious states. This is very much a right brain activity. Children need to be encouraged in this area, because our educational system is biased towards the left brain (Blakeslee, 1980). Although creativity in the arts can function well with little help from the variable left brain processes, most creative work requires healthy cooperation between intuition and logical thought.

Let us put theory aside for a moment and look at the real world of people who have proved to be truly great. Mozart described his apparently subconscious process of musical composition in a famous letter:

> When I feel well and in good humour, or when I am taking a drive or walking after a good meal, or in the night when I cannot sleep, thoughts crowd into my mind as easily as you could wish. Whence and how do they come? I do not know, and I have nothing to do with. Those which please me I keep in my mind and hum them; at least others tell me that I do so. Once I have my theme, another melody comes linking itself to the first one, in accordance with the needs of the composition as a whole: the counterpoint, the part of each instrument, and all those melodic fragments at last produce the entire work.

The sensing attribute involves a high level of mental and physical development resulting in inventions and products in talent areas. However, McAlpine (1988) notes three caveats: (i) not all creative thinkers exhibit all of the traits mentioned; (ii) in themselves these characteristics of thinking and cognitive style do not guarantee creativity – they are predispositions or enabling attributes; (iii) they may have different faces and forms for different age groups.

Researchers such as Torrance (1980) and Getzels and Jackson (1962), who have accepted the broader construct of giftedness, are paying more attention to the importance of imaginative or creative thinking as a major contributor to innovative thought and responsive knowledge production. Most of the psychometric research on gifted populations is primarily concerned with academic achievement or convergent intellectual potentialities, whereas research on creativity frequently has a more secondary status, possibly because of its lack of theory and assessment schemes. Professor Ned Herrmann, in his excellent lecture to the 7th World Conference on gifted and talented children (1987), highlighted the need to take creativity far more seriously and to link the creative brain to mental wholeness, personal uniqueness, change and productivity, which are just a few of the important parameters of creativity and giftedness. Nurturing of this important mental potentiality should be seen not only in the context of differentiated teaching, but also in more general terms, by utilising it in society at large and in education generally. By including children with this particular talent, we have had a broadening effect on attitudes towards the gifted, which is partly responsible for the reduction in charges of elitism. It has also had an impact on both the curriculum and the nature of teaching generally, for a wide range of children in the classroom.

*Creativity test*

It is quite revealing to ask children to write down as many uses of a certain object, such as a brick, bucket or a newspaper. A nine-year-old girl made this list in just ten minutes. This demonstrates fluency and a divergent-thinking child.

> **Uses of a newspaper:** 1. read it; 2. use as a tablecloth; 3. make paper hats with it; 4. draw funny faces on it; 5. make paper aeroplanes; 6. make paper people; 7. make collage; 8. make paper wallets; 9. screw up for use as a projectile; 10. fill in football results; 11. do the crossword; 12. cut out the photographs from it; 13. make dress patterns of it; 14. make a kite with it; 15. make a fire with it; 16. use it as wrapping paper; 17. wrap up fish and chips in it etc., etc.

One of the most important preconditions for creativity to be unleashed is the adequate identification of high, average or low creative potential so that parental, educational, and/or political intervention can reinforce, redirect, revise or even enhance creativity.

> Even though there are already many screening devices on the market, we had reasons to design a more culture-sensitive instrument that assesses creative potentials in most age and ability groups from various educational, socioeconomic, and cultural backgrounds. We also wanted an instrument that was easy to administer, economical in time and cost with a set of evaluation criteria requiring minimal training. (Urban and Jellen, 1996)

Thus, the test should provide a basic set of information which can be used in every creative way possible. In order to avoid culture bias, the researchers used only a drawing task, with no verbal clues (see Figure 3.2). The six figural fragments were intentionally designed in an incomplete fashion with no or only vague conventional meanings in order to achieve a maximum of flexibility as an imperative for creativity. The fragments mirror diverse characteristics that are:

**Figure 3.2:** Urban and Jellen's Test for Creative Thinking–Drawing Production

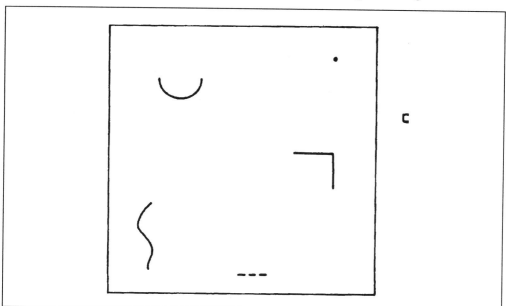

(1) different in design
(2) geometric and nongeometric
(3) round and straight
(4) singular and compositional
(5) broken and unbroken
(6) within and outside a given frame
(7) placed irregularly on the space provided
(8) incomplete

(Urban and Jellen, 1996)

The outcome is the Test for Creative Thinking–Drawing Production (TCT–DP). The first pilot studies revealed that the TCT–DP can indeed identify the level of creative potential in most age and ability groups. The subjects chosen for pilot testing came, however, exclusively from a German cultural background, differing only in the type of schooling received or attended. These first findings were congruent with other research findings on creativity: (1) a moderate group correlation existed between the means of TCT–DP and the academic achievement level of the groups tested; (2) no correlation was seen between individual IQ scores and TCT–DP scores in a group of subjects of relatively homogeneous intellectual calibre. These positive findings with German samples verifying the validity and reliability of the instrument encouraged the researchers to break the ethnocentricity of the database, inviting colleagues from around the world to cooperate in a cross-cultural application of the TCT–DP.

Since practical activities without a theory base are unreliable, the researchers took as their definition of creativity 'the emergence in action of a novel product growing out of the uniqueness of the individual and the materials, events, people or circumstances of the person's life' (Rogers, 1962). The test allows each child to expand, extend, develop and create something that is unique and satisfying to the child, not necessarily to the tester.

The eleven valuation criteria chosen for the test reflect an openness to experience and explore the six fragments in and outside the box. Children are simply asked to complete the picture and give it a title.

I tested 50 ten-year-old children and the most and least creative drawings are reproduced in Figure 3.3. Readers might like to try assessing these on the basis of the criteria above. Questions to consider are:

(1) Are there major differences between genders?

(2) Can the test be applied to children from different countries and cultures?

(3) What does the test tell us about children's creative ability?

## Psychomotor ability

The appeal of the definition of giftedness adopted here is that it recognises not only high general intelligence but also specific talent areas, including psychomotor skills. Terman's (1981) detailed studies of gifted children (Stanford-Binet IQs of 140 plus) showed them to be healthier and better physical specimens. I consider it essential that all talent areas should be identified. Most schools have good facilities for athletes, such as well-equipped sports halls, specialist physical education teachers, considerable individualised learning and a great deal of encouragement and reward. Indeed, the sports programmes in many of our schools could be exemplars of what a gifted programme should be.

In the DES document, *Curriculum 5–16* (1985), Her Majesty's Inspectors state that curricular physical education should include five areas of experience: 'to promote skilful body management; 'participation in creative, artistic activities requiring expressive movement; competition between groups or individuals involving the use of psychomotor skills; activities leading to increased suppleness, mobility, strength and stamina; and challenging experiences in various environments.' This classification is close to the description of sport offered in the *European 'Sport for All' Charter* (Sports Council, 1976) which linked physical education in schools with outside community agencies responsible for sport, dance and physical recreation generally. This division is important because, although schools have reasonable facilities and well-trained teachers

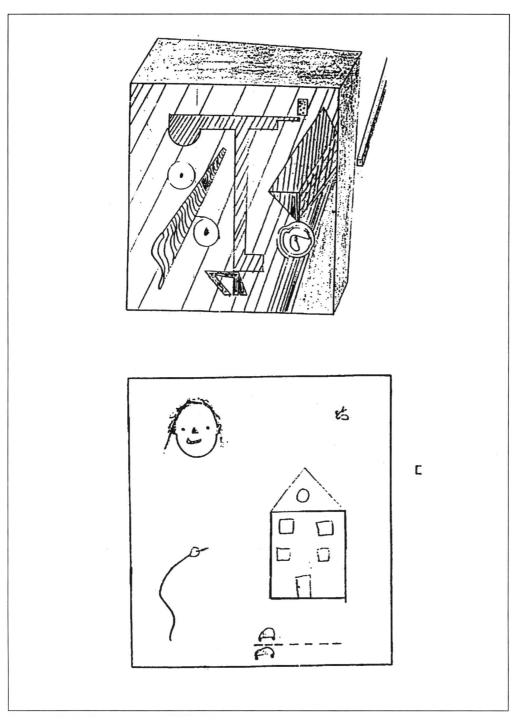

**Figure 3.3:** Examples of TCT–DP drawings

in physical education, outside community facilities and encouragement from experts are very much a part of the extension necessary for our young people.

My own philosophy has been greatly influenced by the ideas of Carolyn Jones of Newcastle-upon-Tyne University, who deems the aims of physical education to be:

(1) the physical development of each person;
(2) the development of the whole person in society through physical activities;
(3) the promotion of excellence and life-long participation in physical activity.

This philosophy respects, within the framework of society, the individuality of human growth and development and the uniqueness of each person. It also encapsulates what Parry (1977) refers to as 'qualitarianism' or excellence on the one hand and 'egalitarianism' or sport for all on the other. Each enriches the other and quality is the prize: quality in human endeavour; quality in education; and quality of life. This perspective receives some support from the DES:

> Provision of physical education, like that for other aspects of education, must be planned with the needs of all young people in mind. Every child should have the option to take part in sport at a level appropriate to his ability and existing resources should allow him that opportunity. (DES, 1978)

The Sports Council (1984) suggests that the aim is not just a form of national and world class championships, for few attain these heights, but encouragement for each individual to achieve their own level and fulfil their own potential. The Sports Council recognises that there are differential levels of achievement and that, as a result, success in psychomotor ability is both relative and a matter of degree. This interpretation of 'excellence' incorporates the full ability range, as well as including all forms of psychomotor ability. This gets over the criticism that the concept of excellence should not be elitist. It is a matter of developing each person's physical skills to the full potential.

The nature and range of physical skills that should be developed in children have been well documented, and have been prescribed quite closely by the Physical Education Committee of HMI (personal communication, 1979). These skills include perception, decision making, control of movement, evaluation, physical skills, skills of posture and orientation, fine manipulative skills, gross motor skills, artistic skills and communication skills. Within the five areas of experience identified by the DES, the following activities should be encouraged: gymnastics, games, athletics, swimming and general outdoor pursuits.

The DES (1977) confirms Ogilvie's (1973) findings that exceptional performers are easily identifiable by their achievements and that performance in many physical activities is quantifiable. However, the identification of outstanding potential is more problematic, possibly because of the difficulty in distinguishing between early maturation and exceptional ability; the problem of catering for the late developer; the diversity of physical activities; the fact that psychomotor ability may be unitary or multi-faceted; the dependence of psychomotor ability upon opportunity. Nevertheless, experienced teachers and others should be able to recognise the attributes of strength, endurance, suppleness, agility, coordination, rhythm, harmonious movement, balance and economy of effort.

The aim of developing whole people is consistent with the World Health Organisation's definition of health, which is a 'state of complete physical, mental and social well-being, not merely the absence of disease and infirmity'. Furthermore, if we believe that a healthy body equals a healthy mind, then physical education has a vital role in developing in young people the power to live a full, adult life.

There is a growing interest in the idea that we can all take more responsibility for our own health and a recognition that good health is more than freedom from disease or infirmity. The idea of a holistic living programme is now the fastest-growing and most important development in the domain of health and healing. It is a programme of self-care in which a person is seen as a whole-body, mind and spirit, with each part interrelated. Despite the tendency in education to develop the cognitive areas of a child to the detriment of the cultural, physical and the spiritual dimensions, we need to believe strongly in the concept of a healthy mind and a healthy body and, therefore, PE needs protection and support.

## Visual and performing arts

This area of the curriculum is under considerable pressure because the National Curriculum puts greater weight on English, mathematics and science, which are largely left brain activities. Yet it is vitally important that the whole curriculum for the whole child should include the aesthetic areas of a child's education. The following lists characterise children with potential talents in art, drama and music:

*Art*

- demonstrate vivid imagination
- remember great detail
- draw a great variety of things and not just flowers, houses and people
- have a long attention span for art activities, including planning the composition of their work well
- are delighted to try out different materials, media and techniques
- are keen observers of the world around them (though this applies to scientists as well)

- set high standards and often re-work their creation to achieve these ends
- take art activities very seriously and derive great satisfaction from them – this includes showing interest in other children's creations.

## Drama

- are adept at improvising, imitation and role-play
- are often lithe, and can handle their bodies with ease and poise
- show great interest in dramatic activities and often volunteer for plays and sketches
- often relate stories with effective use of gestures and facial expressions – watch their body language
- create original work
- can create suspense and easily relate stories that evoke emotional responses from their listeners
- can hold the attention of the class and get others to respond well.

## Music

- obviously enjoy and seek out musical activities and take every opportunity to hear and create music
- may play a musical instrument or express a strong desire to do so from an early age
- often have perfect pitch
- make up original tunes
- can easily remember and reproduce melodies and rhythm patterns
- are knowledgeable about background sounds, chords and individual instruments
- respond sensitively to music by body movements and mood changes.

## Leadership

In general, students who are more articulate, better adjusted and more socially adaptable seem to be rated high on leadership qualities. Here are a few leadership roles:

- taking action
- encouraging the less able
- being observant and sensitive to people
- having a sense of humour and making life enjoyable
- having a preference for innovation
- influencing other children's behaviour
- being rigorous and persistent
- having self confidence and a good self-concept

- setting a good example
- controlling and unifying
- making policy
- good planning
- pooling and focusing ideas
- achieving a goal
- identifying a need
- providing expertise
- taking responsibility

Plowman (1981) itemised six aspects of leadership in the form of adjectives: charismatic, intuitive, generative, analytical, evaluative and synergistic. Chapter 4 will include leadership education. We can teach children about the characteristics of leadership and how to be a good leader, as well as placing them in leadership situations in order to enhance this particular talent area.

## RECOGNISING TALENT BY THE QUALITY OF WORK CHILDREN PRODUCE

Possibly the best way to recognise high ability in any aspect of school work is the actual performance of children. Several examples of children's work follow, covering different subjects and ages of children (see pp.52–5).

There are at least two questions both parents and teachers should consider when looking at this work:

(1)  What level of ability is this child at?
(2)  How would you extend these children to help them reach their potential?

Of course, parents should know their children better than any teacher possibly can. This is particularly important in the early crucial years when parents will note when children start to talk, to ask questions and to read. Unfortunately, some schools do not ask parents enough about their children before they come to school. If we believe that parents are the most important teacher a child ever has, then schools really should ask parents to participate more in the enabling curriculum. The following Parent Questionnaire (see p.56) is recommended so that a child starting school can be given appropriate educational experiences at the correct level for that child. A biographical and developmental history summarising the child's early development in order to identify past obstacles or boosts to learning in the child's health, home, culture and previous educational history would be most helpful for any teacher. Later in their school career a simple questionnaire for children to complete would help to build up a comprehensive profile of the child.

Regretfully, some parents do not know their children well or understand their gifts, talents and precocity; whereas others overestimate their children's abilities. This is where cooperation between school and home is important. This will be discussed in Chapter 6.

A topic on dinosaur's by six year old infants. The teacher asked the children how the could solve the problem of cleaning a dinosaur's teeth. This is Daniel's creative solution.

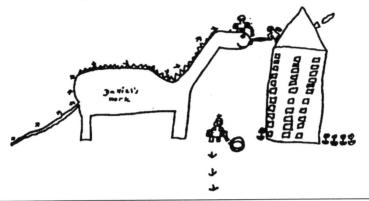

A man climbs the dinosaur's back to its head, where he dangles food in front of its eyes to open its mouth. Another person on the house-roof cleans the dinosaur's teeth with a brush. The person on the ground is putting glue down to keep the dinosaur still. He is wearing a mask because the glue is poisonous .

Daniel

UP IN SPACE.

I am in a space capsule, and I am landing on a big planet with craters in it and it is very cold. I can jump very high and I landed in a crater. There are funny green animals here. There is no one else here except me. I have a space buggy and I drive around space in it. I went on an exploration and found funny flowers with spikes on. They have pink leaves. I was so lonely that I went home.

THE END.

By Karen ·-;··· Age 5½

Notice the skills of writing, the language, knowledge, humour and the human touches at the end.

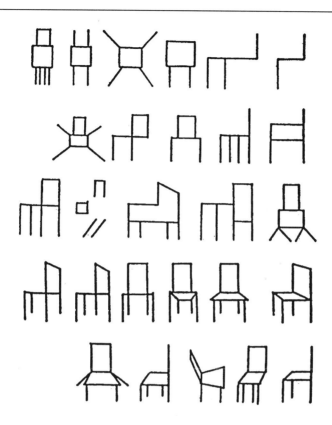

In a craft lesson the class were asked to draw a chair from as many angles as possible. Susan, aged 14, whose father is an architect, produced 17 drawings.

Elizabeth, aged 12, took a different approach from the rest of her class when they were asked to write an essay on 'conflict'.

## Conflict Surprise (a receipt for war)

*Ingredients:*

5 kg of greed
2 kg of envy
1 raw anger
1 large selfish (very ripe)
5 g of mistrust
7 kg of over-ripe violence
3 large misunderstandings
(if you have them)

*Method:*

Using a fist, mix in the greed and envy, let it simmer for an hour. Kick the raw anger in. Squeeze the selfish and add it to thicken the mixture. Sprinkle in the mistrust and stir thoroughly. Using a tank (if you have one) fire in the violence. Beat in the misunderstandings, take a world leader and empty its mind of peaceful thoughts. Using half the mixture refill the mind. Carefully put the world leader back in its place. Using a sword spread the other half of the mixture across one of the world's countries. Remember to stand back after you have done this; you may become a victim of your own creation. Watch for the after effects, you will enjoy the pain and suffering. You will find it impossible to clean the kitchen when you have finished; all the ingredients will contaminate the rest of the kitchen. Quick tip. For fuller flavour, act first, think later.

A pen and ink drawing by Imran who was 13 years old. The hand is a most difficult part of the body to draw.

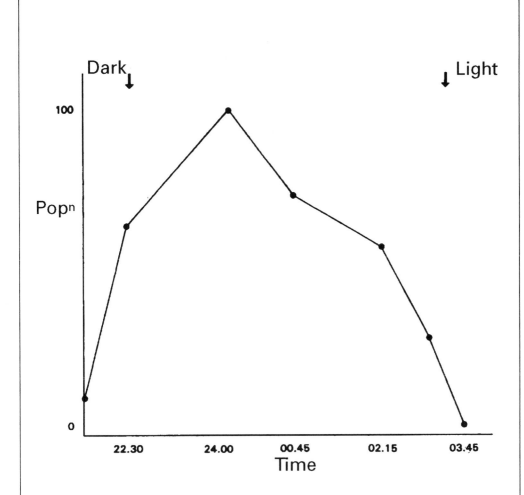

At a Saturday school for gifted children, all of whom had been nominated by their teachers as children who would benefit from being extended, the author did a 2-hour workshop based on woodlice. As a result two 9-year-old boys (David and Sean) stayed up all night counting woodlice on a garden wall. This is their result which proves woodlice are strictly nocturnal.

# PARENT QUESTIONNAIRE

*Child's name:* ................................................................................................

Place a tick on the line to indicate how you, honestly, rate the characteristic as listed in your child for his or her age level. (A wide range of possible characteristics is provided, and it would be unrealistic to assume that any one child would be high in all categories.)

| Characteristic | RATING SCALE | | |
| --- | --- | --- | --- |
| | Average | High | Exceptional |
| 1. Concentration (has ability to concentrate, not easily distracted) | | | |
| 2. Knowledge and skills (a wide knowledge of basic skills and factual information, a high level of understanding) | | | |
| 3. Enjoyment of learning | | | |
| 4. Persistence (has ability and desire to stay with a difficult task until it is done, likes competition, not easily distracted) | | | |
| 5. Intellectual curiosity (pursues interests primarily to understand and to satisfy curiosity, questions the ordinary or the unusual, generates questions of his/her own) | | | |
| 6. Acceptance of a challenge (enjoys the challenge of difficult problems, tasks, issues and materials) | | | |
| 7. Perceptiveness (is alert, perceptive and observant beyond his/her years, aware of many stimuli) | | | |
| 8. Verbal facility (shows marked facility with language, uses words easily and accurately, wide vocabulary) | | | |
| 9. Fluency of ideas (produces a large number of products and ideas, often very quickly) | | | |

| Characteristic | RATING SCALE Average | High | Exceptional |
|---|---|---|---|
| 10. Flexibility (approaches ideas and problems from a number of perspectives, finds alternative ways of solving problems) | | | |
| 11. Originality (often uses original methods of solving problems, can combine ideas and materials in a variety of ways) | | | |
| 12. Reasoning (is logical, often generalises or applies understanding in new situations, expands concepts into broader relationships) | | | |
| 13. Independence in thought (inclined to follow his/her own organisation and ideas rather than the structuring of others) | | | |
| 14. Independence and work habits (requires minimum of adult direction and attention) | | | |
| 15. Independence in action (can plan and organise activities, direct action) | | | |
| 16. Aesthetic appreciation (enjoys and is responsive to beauty in the arts and/or nature) | | | |
| 17. Can produce 'reasons' which may be elaborate for not doing things in the usual way | | | |

Please add any other characteristics:

Form completed by: ............................................................................................

Date ........................................................................

# STUDENT QUESTIONNAIRE

Read each statement below. Think carefully about yourself. Write a brief comment by the statement if it sounds like you. Complete the questionnaire as fully as possible. Add anything you wish on the reverse side.

*Student's name:*..................................................................................................

School:................................................................................................................

---

1. Areas and skills which are easiest in school

---

2. Areas and skills which are hardest in school

---

3. Things enjoyed most

---

4. Things not enjoyed (areas disliked or in which change is desired)

---

5. Areas or activities in which greatest progress is felt

---

6. Preference for working conditions alone, with others, long periods, where, etc.)

---

7. Sports and games (what activities, evaluation of progress, with whom)

In school

Out of school

---

8. Use of free time (activities, with whom)

At school

At home

---

9. Areas in which 'creative' products and freedom of expression are especially enjoyed (writing, music, art, speaking, dance, physical education, drama, construction/manipulative, etc.)

---

10. Hobbies and favourite recreation, collections, can you organise things in unusual ways?

---

11. Lessons out of school – special opportunities

---

12. Television habits:

Types of programmes preferred

Frequency of viewing

---

13. Reading habits:

Kinds of material preferred

Amount of time spent reading

---

14. Special responsibilities or jobs out of school

---

15. Clubs and organisations (special friends who belong, activity leadership role, offices held or desired, etc.)

---

16. Activities in which family participates as a group

---

17. Possible vocational choices

---

18. Educational ambitions

---

19. I like my work to be perfect

---

20. Problems encountered

---

21. I am able to explain things using examples

---

# ADVANTAGES AND DISADVANTAGES OF VARIOUS METHODS OF IDENTIFICATION

| Method | Use and limitations |
| --- | --- |
| *Teacher observation/judgement* | Teacher judgement is questionable yet essential. The trained eyes of teachers should know their children but they may miss those who do not conform to accepted standards of work or behaviour, children with motivational or emotional problems or with belligerent or apathetic attitudes, or children from homes that do not share the school's ethos and where there are low expectations. |
| *Checklists* | Useful as a quick guide to what to look out for; may |

| | |
|---|---|
| | not be relevant for individual cases. Should involve parents; e.g. the Infant Checklist should be part of the baseline assessment of children starting school. Some parents are reluctant to have their children labelled and therefore downgrade them; others may overestimate their child's ability. |
| *General and specific checklists* | Can be misleading, unreliable and lack valid data. Time needed to train teachers, but quick to administer. |
| *Peer nomination* | Children know who is best at a subject as well as knowing what their outside interests are. |
| *Intelligence tests* | Can be useful as an initial screen to supplement and counterbalance teacher observations, and time efficient. May not identify those with motivational or emotional problems; with reading difficulties or those from different ethnic/cultural backgrounds. |
| *Achievement test batteries* | Helpful in providing more detailed information on a wider range of skills, but subject to some limitations as group tests. Time-consuming for teachers. Will not necessarily identify the true abilities of children nor leadership or social skills. |
| *Creativity tests* | May offer chance to show quality of imagination and divergent thinking in those overlooked by conventional tests above. Difficult to assess, define and measure, and time-consuming to administer. |
| *Individual intelligence tests* | Provide more accurate and reliable information on ability to 'reason' in conventional terms and directly related to identification. May not indicate how a child will perform in class, nor predict achievement in individual cases. Costly in use of time and subject to cultural bias. |
| *Nomination* | Useful information especially from parents to build up a profile. |
| *Renzulli's rating scales* | Well researched, well constructed and tried but no cut offs given. |
| *Creative learning environments* | The all-important ingredient, encouraging all children to explore their talents; exercise their developing capacity to learn and understand; and to reach the highest potential of which they are capable if they are given the opportunity. |
| *Tests on specific ability* | An attempt to measure difficult constructs such as artistic, unusual or scientific ability. Limited in scope and general lack of information regarding validity. |

Remember also: school grades; interview and anecdotal records; student interest inventories; student products (see the examples of quality work, which are all at least one Key Stage ahead of what one would expect at that age).

## Which test for which students?

The following matrix may help to determine what procedures a school might use. The vertical axis is divided into three broad categories – test data, performance data and developmental data – which are each subdivided into types of tests.
Talent areas are listed on the horizontal axis.

| | | Academic/ intellectual skills | Artistic/ expressive skills | Leadership/ psychosocial skills | Divergent production/ process skills | Kinesthetic/expressive & manipulative skills |
|---|---|---|---|---|---|---|
| TEST DATA | Intelligence | * | | | | |
| | Achievement | * | | | | |
| | Creatively divergent thinking | • | * • | | * • | |
| | Aptitude | * • | • | * | • | * |
| | Divergent feeling | | * | | * | |
| | Biographical inventory | * | * • | * • | | |
| | Culture free | • | | | | |
| PERFORMANCE DATA | Grades | * | | | | |
| | Demonstration of skills | * • | * • | * • | * • | * • |
| | Teacher and/or school personnel | * | * • | * • | * • | * • |
| | Peer | * • | * • | * • | * • | * • |
| | Parent | * • | * • | | * • | * • |
| | Self | * • | * • | * • | * • | * • |
| DEVELOPMENTAL DATA | Case studies | * • | * • | * • | * • | * • |
| | Anecdotes | * • | * • | * • | * • | * • |
| | Biographical data | * • | * • | * • | * • | * • |
| | Interviews | * • | * • | * • | * • | * • |

\* represents measures that should be used in the identification of mainstream gifted children.
• represents measures that should be used in the identification of culturally different gifted children.

# CHAPTER 4

# Provision and Strategies for Teaching

> The education of the child shall be directed to the development of the child's
> personality, talents and mental and physical abilities to their fullest potential.
> (The United Nations Convention on the Rights of the Child, Article 29)

## MODELS OF PROVISION

There are various methods of providing for our gifted and talented children. Before adopting a model, it is advisable to consider the following questions:

(1) Does the method properly emphasise the acquisition of a higher order of thinking skills and concepts?
(2) Is the method flexible and open-ended enough for the child to develop at his or her own pace?
(3) Does the method provide a learning environment as emotionally protected as it is intellectually stimulating?
(4) Is the method likely to alienate a child from his or her peer group and will it be detrimental to the child's subsequent learning, introducing factors that will inevitably be repeated later which could lead to boredom?
(5) Does the method provide a process that is valuable to the child, rather than a product that is prestigious for the school?

Davis and Rimm (1989) suggest that a model can provide a useful theoretical framework within which enriched activities can be planned. In their excellent book they cover ten models, which range from the detailed and specific revolving door identification model (Renzulli et al., 1981) to models that have more general suggestions for skill and development goals and activities. Space does not allow a detailed description of these models, but briefly they are as follows:

(1) **The Enrichment Triad Model** (Renzulli, 1977) lends itself to self-contained classroom adaptation. This model includes three enrichment types. Type 1 offers general exploratory activities, and is intended to expose students to a great many topics. Type 2 is enrichment in group training activities and tries to teach analytical, critical, creative and evaluative thinking, as well as good self-concept, values and, motivation as well as library and research skills. Type 3 enrichment consists of individual and small group investigations of real problems. This type is most appropriate for the most able children.

(2) **The Revolving Door Identification Model** (Renzulli et al., 1981) is a complete programming guide. It proposes a talent pool of 15–20 per cent of any school population. All talent pool students receive types 1 and 2 enrichment, and the most able students move into a resource room to work on projects.

(3) **The Multiple Menu Model** (Renzulli, 1988) is a series of five planning guides that suggest sequences and alternatives for teaching content efficiently.

(4) **The Pyramid Project** (Cox et al., 1985) is a three-level plan intended to overcome many criticisms of gifted and talented programmes, especially the popular pull-out plan used in the USA. Above-average students are mainstreamed in the normal classroom, more able students are placed in full-time special classes, and the most able students of all attend magnet or residential schools.

(5) **The Three-Stage Enrichment Model** (Feldhusen and Kolloff, 1981) focuses mainly on fostering creative thinking, but also on independent learning skills, research and positive self-concepts. The programme is developmental in that stage 1 involves short-term teacher-led exercises in creative, critical and logical thinking, stage 2 involves more complex thinking, and stage 3 activities focus on independent learning by challenging students to define the problem, gather information and creatively report their findings.

(6) **The Guilford and Meeker Structure of Intellect Model** (Guilford, 1967, 1977; Meeker and Meeker, 1986) is a rather complex theory of intelligence based upon 120 combinations of 5 operations, 6 products and 4 contents. Meeker uses 26 abilities from the Guilford Model to guide and diagnose specific learning abilities, especially those related to creativity, mathematics, reading and writing. This approach can be useful in identifying a gifted minority and disadvantaged students.

(7) **Treffinger's Model** (Treffinger, 1975) is a four-stage model to increase self-directedness. The four stages are: the command style, which is teacher-directed; the task style, in which students select from teacher-prepared activities; the peer-partner style, which enables students to make more decisions about learning goals and activities; and the self-directed style, whereby a student creates the choices, makes the selections and chooses the amount of working time.

(8) **The Autonomous Learner Model** (Betts, 1985) fits 'usage within the classroom'. This programming guide includes five dimensions of orientating students and others to giftedness and to the content and purposes of the programme. This also involves individual development in areas of learning skills, personal understanding, interpersonal skills, student enrichment activities, as well as career development.

(9) **The Williams Model** (Williams, 1970) develops thinking and feeling processes. The eighteen teaching strategies may be classified according to the three categories of the enrichment triad model.

(10) **The Taylor Multiple Talent Totem Pole Model** (Taylor, 1978) states that learning activities focus upon developing academic ability, creativity, communicating, predicting, organising, decision making and evaluation.

Open-ended teaching/learning models can be used with all students to build confidence and to individualise the learning experience.

(1) **Bloom's taxonomy** (Bloom, 1974) assumes that learning proceeds through a number of stages:

*Knowledge:* knowing and remembering
*Comprehension:* understanding
*Application:* applying what you know
*Analysis:* analysing what you know
*Synthesis:* combining what you know
*Evaluation:* judging the outcome

Activities can be planned to respond to each of the stages, encouraging a broader approach to the topic. Note that the upper levels are especially appropriate for the gifted.

(2) **Creative learning contracts** (Megarrity) integrate learning activities across subject areas. They can be based on student or teacher interests.

*Content:* What are the major concepts to be studied?
*Skills:* Which learning-to-learn skills are to be practised? Which critical or creative thinking skills are to be included?
*Learning activities:* These are to be completed independently or cooperatively by students with the minimum of teacher input. Students become responsible for their own learning.

(3) **De Bono's six hat thinking model** (de Bono, 1985) is a scaffolding model, using parallel thinking to focus on an issue or problem.

*White hat:* the thinker focuses on the 'pure 'facts.
*Red hat:* the thinker switches to a 'feeling' mode, using intuition, senses or emotions without justifying.
*Black hat:* the thinker may ask negative questions or point out errors.
*Yellow hat:* the thinker is constructive, considering benefits.
*Green hat:* the thinker considers alternatives.
*Blue hat:* the thinker monitors thinking, using this for planning.

These models may be helpful in making a decision about what programme to propose for any group of students in any single school. The thoughtful teacher will consider all of these models, along with more specific strategies such as enrichment, which will be discussed later. For the purposes of this book, I shall investigate further four of the categories that Ogilvie (1973) proposed as talent areas. First, however, a few comments about individual studies.

## Individual studies

The use of individual studies allows the curriculum to develop out of students' own interests. Children are obviously motivated to do better on a topic if it comes from their own interests. They are also able to take ownership for their own learning and to do good research. Teachers have a responsibility to see that the students understand the basic steps in preparing their research and topic report – choosing the subject, planning, outlining, gathering information from a variety of sources, writing, revising and preparing the final report. Another factor is the opportunity for students to work with people who have a like enthusiasm and knowledge related to their choice of subject. Teachers have to be humble enough to ask an expert in the school to mentor a student, or to ask for support from outside experts in the community. This should be encouraged, because no teacher can know all there is to know about any one subject, and outstanding children need the stimulus that may be acquired only from someone with a depth of knowledge that an average teacher cannot possibly have.

Let us now consider the four talent areas in our definition.

# CREATIVITY

One of the goals of gifted education is to develop creative and imaginative thinking, as well as problem solving, in order to encourage gifted students to function as creative and productive people in their society. Encouragement comes from the provision of appropriate learning environments and learning experiences, designed for the production of ideas that reflect growth from the known to the original. The learning experiences should integrate cognitive skills, affective skills, intuition and talents in a specific area.

Recommendations for creative teaching include: teacher enthusiasm, encouraging self-initiated projects, acceptance of individual differences in our children, the encouragement of divergent thinking, and certainly looking beyond IQ scores. Creative learning can result in higher achievement, improved motivation, greater self-confidence and a better attitude towards school.

Although there is still some difficulty in defining the concept of creativity, many researchers have tried to make the term more tangible by identifying specific creative abilities (Guilford, 1967; Torrance, 1980; Davis and Rimm, 1989), and the most widely quoted four are:

**Fluency** – the ability to generate many solutions or alternatives. For example:

> Think of several possible ways to –
> Come up with ideas for –
> List as many ways to –

**Flexibility** – thinking in a variety of categories and taking several approaches. For example:

> Think of different kinds of reasons for –
> List as many different ways to –
> What are the different kinds of –

**Originality** – the ability to arrive at novel, unusual, non-conforming conclusions. For example:

> Think of unique and unusual ways to –
> Think of ideas no one else will think of –

**Elaboration** – the ability to add details and develop ideas. For example:

> Think of details to develop your main idea.
>
> Add supplementary ideas to make the basic idea clearer

These creative abilities are very much encouraged in future problem-solving activities and the 'odyssey of the mind' programmes in the USA. Units of instruction such as the study of inventions and inventing itself excite and challenge gifted students, while tapping into their innovative spirit.

**Creative activities** (some suggested activities I have used over the years)

*Living on a sand-dune*
In science, one area of interest for gifted children is: What does it mean to be alive? After some initial discussion about life processes and the characteristics of all living things, the children will soon realise that these life processes are carried out in many diverse ways. The following activity enables the children to design their own organism, remembering that a sand-dune is a tough environment in which to survive.

Activity

(1) Create an organism that can survive and perform all life functions on a dry, windblown and mobile sand-dune.
(2) Your three-dimensional organism can be made of any materials using common household items.
(3) You will be asked to present your organism to the class, and justify its design one week from today.

Evaluation
This is based on how well the life functions can be carried out, remembering the limiting properties of the organism's environment.

*A tall structure* (science, maths, design technology)

Overview
At times, students should be encouraged to practise generating ideas beyond the norm. Challenging, problem-solving activity gives them the opportunity to approach a problem in a new way.

Activity

(1) Work in groups of two or three and design and build the tallest freestanding structure possible using readily available household and basic classroom materials.
(2 Each group should be given one sheet of paper, some sellotape and scissors.

It would be a good idea for the small groups of children to discuss their plan of action before construction commences. This teaches cooperation in groups.
   Creative activity often appears to be simply a special problem-solving activity characterised by novelty. Here are just a few suggestions:

(1) If you were king of the castle, what would you do if your serfs went on strike?
(2) List all the qualities you look for in a friend. Which is the most important? Why?
(3) List all the reasons you can think of for eating vegetables.
(4) Think of several colloquial expressions, for example 'a hole in one', or 'down in the mouth', or 'a pain in the neck'. Illustrate, and elaborate on each expression.
(5) Pretend you are a fashion designer and predict what the new fashion will be in the year 2000. Think of as many original fads as you can and pick out your favourite.

Creativity is the ability to see, to be aware and to respond. Here are some examples:

(1) You are probably aware that the rings in a tree trunk help determine the age of the tree. The tree trunk, however, also twists axially as it grows. Brainstorm to find reasons why this may occur, and also what phenomena it might help us to understand.
(2) Create a sound map of your school.
(3) Mrs Jones has been left 46 cats in her aunt's will. She is at a loss what to do with these felines, yet she will lose £100,000 if she gives the cats away without checking each potential owner out most thoroughly. List as many ways as possible for dealing with all these cats.

   Originality is simply a fresh pair of eyes. Here are some examples to encourage this:

(1) Write a poem that describes your personality and includes your name.
(2) Describe what a television set sees as it sits and watches you.
(3) With the invention of CDs, records have become obsolete. Name all the things you could do with your out-dated record collection.
(4) Think of as many reasons as you can for recycling waste materials from your home and school, and list how they could be re-used.
(5) List 25 ways to keep you from being bored in school, at home or on a long car journey.
(6) Five new planets have just been discovered. Think of different names for these planets and give reasons for choosing the names.
(7) A teacher or parent could collect unusual headlines from newspapers or magazines, or better still, encourage the children to bring them to school. The more unusual or potentially humourous the headline, the better.
   Children are then randomly assigned a different headline and asked to write a brief new article on what they think the headline is about. The children should be encouraged to use fluency, flexibility and originality in coming up with their ideas, as well as elaboration in fleshing out the story.

**Creative questions**

Teachers and parents can use the art of questioning creatively in the classroom and at home. Creative questioning, skilfully employed, causes students to develop both their sense of wonder and their communication skills, though they should always be given plenty of time to think of imaginative responses. Such questions could be as follows:

(1) How many uses can you think of for a....?
(2) What would happen if there were no....?
(3) What could you do to improve a....?
(4) How might you feel if you were a....?

Ask children to make creative choices and ask them to say why. For example:

(1) Would you rather be the wind or a river?
(2) Would you rather be a bird or a cat?
(3) Would you rather be the Prime Minister or a Liverpool football player?

The creative process is any thinking process which solves a problem in an original and useful way.

## LEADERSHIP

In our definition, any field of human endeavour is represented by its leaders, including the creative arts, technology, research, exploration, a business, a church or a sports team. Definitions of leadership usually amount to a list of characteristics and skills, and these include: confidence, being well regarded, adaptability, high responsibility, skills in communication, planning, group dynamics and public relations.

It is the duty of teachers to encourage the special talent of leadership, which some children possess. Leadership education can include teaching students about leadership styles by looking at biographies of great leaders; teaching the skills of leadership; putting students into a leadership role; as well as teaching them the skills of communication, planning, problem solving and decision making. Magoon (1981) described five leadership activities: mentorship, in-school leadership projects, community projects, simulations and classroom monitors. These involve the teacher in providing the opportunity by having a creative learning environment which was discussed earlier.

**What makes a leader?** (suggested exercises)

An attempt to produce a profile of leadership characteristics, listing such qualities as bravery, integrity and charisma, can be the basis of a profitable discussion, although it may not be easy to agree what these things mean. In discussing leadership, a number of questions might be asked, including:

(1)  Do leaders lead every group they join?
(2)  Are leaders more interested in themselves than others?
(3)  Is it possible for a loner to be a leader?
(4)  Are leaders created by situations?
(5)  Are leaders achievers or exponents of excellence?
(6)  Do leaders operate through fear?
(7)  Do groups accept leaders because they help to get what the group wants?
(8)  Do leaders really persuade groups that they want what the leader wants?

The following leadership portraits may help children to consider how leaders differ from each other and how some characteristics may be common to them all.

*Bob Geldof*

Bob Geldof was born in 1954 in Dublin. His mother died when he was very young. After a number of casual jobs he went to Canada as a pop music journalist. Returning to Dublin in 1979 he and some friends formed the highly successful Boomtown Rats pop group.

When he saw newsfilm of starving Ethiopians in 1984, he was so moved that he decided he must do something to raise money to help these people. He persuaded over fifty musicians, record producers and others to make a single, *Do They Know it's Christmas?* It sold 3 million copies in Britain alone and raised £8 million worldwide for Ethiopia. Bob then had the idea of 'The Global Jukebox'. The 'Live

Aid' concert which followed created sixteen hours of live entertainment that reached 80 per cent of the world's TV sets and raised over £50 million.

Bob is continuing with other campaigns. 'It is important to make a grand gesture, so that you can focus the attention of governments. We have kept millions of people alive. Now we must give them life... this means more money for long-term projects.'

- What particular leadership qualities do you think Bob Geldof possesses?
- Do you think it accurate to describe him as a 'media hero'?
- In what ways do you think that being a pop star helped Bob Geldof to influence people?
- What do you think people will remember about Bob Geldof in fifty years time?

*Martin Luther King*

Martin Luther King was born in 1929 in the American South, living against a background of poverty, racial discrimination and the terror of the Ku Klux Klan. As a young Baptist minister in Alabama he became involved in the Civil Rights movement. Only eight years later he led a great Civil Rights march to Washington in which over 200,000 people, black and white, took part. It was in his speech at the Lincoln Memorial that he challenged America with his famous declaration: 'I have a dream that one day this nation will rise up, live out the true meaning of its creed . . . that all men are equal.'

In the same year, King was awarded the Nobel Peace Prize of £10,000. He gave it all to the cause of Civil Rights. Throughout his life he preached against violence of all kinds. He opposed America's part in the Vietnam War. His work was bitterly attacked in many parts of the USA. Civil Rights workers, black and white, were beaten or murdered. 'Every man should have something to die for. A man who won't die for something isn't fit to live.'

At the age of 38, on a motel balcony in Memphis, Tennessee, Martin Luther King was shot dead by white extremist James Earl Ray.

- What part do you think that race and place of birth played in making Martin Luther King a leader?
- Do you think that being a church minister helped or hindered his campaign?
- King was a great orator. How important is oratory to leadership?
- What do you think kept him going in times of hardship and danger?

*Florence Nightingale*

Florence Nightingale's parents christened her after the Italian city where she was born. As she grew up, they thought she was a quiet child who worried and brooded too much. They were not pleased when she announced that she wanted to take up the poorly regarded task of nursing the sick. Nevertheless, at the age of twenty-four, she began a ten-year study of nursing practices in

England and Europe, becoming convinced that there was a need for women with a sense of vocation to take up the work. Her first job was the little sought one of matron in a mental hospital.

In 1854, when she heard about the terrible conditions of the wounded British soldiers in the Crimean War, she offered to lead a party of women nurses to work in the Military Hospital at Scutari. There she found appalling conditions. The wounded, lying in disease-ridden squalor, died of fever rather than their wounds. She was ruthless in the use of her links with influential people, completely overhauling the Army medical services and reducing the hospital death rate by over 40 per cent. Soldiers blessed the 'lady with the lamp' who overcame resistance from officials to obtain the supplies and improvements that she saw were needed.

Returning to London amid public acclaim in 1856, she set up the Nightingale Training School for Nurses at St Thomas's Hospital. Using money collected by public subscription, she raised the status of nursing and created a new kind of nurse who took the 'Nightingale' method all over the world.

- What obstacles did Florence Nightingale have to overcome?
- What qualities of leadership did she show?
- How similar was her life to that of other upper class women of her time?
- Do you think you would have been able to work under her leadership?
- Are there any causes today that need a new 'Florence Nightingale'?

*Mother Teresa*

In 1910 a little girl called Agnes was born in Yugoslavia. By the time she was twelve, her Christian upbringing led her to feel that God had a particular purpose for her. Her wish to join the Loretto Order of Nuns who taught in Calcutta was fulfilled when she was sent to the Loretto Abbey in Dublin in 1928. As Sister Teresa, she taught geography at St Mary's High School in Calcutta. Every day she saw poor and sick people who lived, slept and died in the streets in conditions that were often worse than those provided for animals. She decided that in order to help these people she had to live amongst them.

In 1946, she was granted permission by the Pope to live outside the Convent with the slum people of Calcutta and was trained as a nurse by the American Missionary Sisters. By 1950, Mother Teresa and her helpers (among whom were doctors and nurses) had formed the Missionaries of Charity. Food and money were sent to Centres all over the world for the relief of the sick and for the care of poor, unwanted and abandoned children. At her request, a new group, the Missionary Brothers of Charity, was formed. They opened homes for the physically and mentally handicapped, as well as schools, youth centres and health clinics. An international appeal spread the work across the world.

In 1979, Mother Teresa was awarded the Nobel Peace Prize. Today, she still travels the world encouraging her co-workers, but she always returns to the slums of Calcutta.

- Some people seem to have the ability to attract the help of others. Why do you think this is so?
- Not everyone can devote all their energies to a single purpose. Can you think of others who have?
- Where do you think Mother Teresa found the strength for her work?

## Leadership characteristics

A leader:

- recognises a need;
- achieves a goal;
- takes action;
- takes responsibility;
- provides expertise;
- sets an example;
- encourages the less able;
- pools and focuses ideas;
- controls and unifies;
- plans;
- creates policy.

Having looked at biographies of great leaders and having listed their characteristics, it would be an idea to extend this activity by then looking at power structures or spheres of influence operating in any classroom or youth group to find out who are the most influential members of the class or group, and when their influence is greatest. It would also be profitable to consider the differences between leaders and managers (see Figure 4.1)

## Projects for potential leaders

In everyday life people may be thrown into situations that call for leadership, in which they must think ahead, establish priorities, make decisions, keep their nerve, persuade others to follow a course of action. There are no absolutely right answers in such situations, but some actions may be better than others. Here are some decision-making exercises.

### Rescue

You and two friends are on the way to school. You are surprised to find letters blowing about the pavement from an open post office pillar box. Not far away, just around the corner, beside his van, lies the postman. He is not moving. What would be the first thing you would tell your friends to do? What would you do? What would you not do? Make a list of actions in the order that they should be taken.

*The nature of leadership*

| Leadership | vs. | Management |
|---|---|---|
| Pull | | Push |
| Empower | | Control |
| Long-term vision | | Short-term goals |
| Group intelligence | | Single intelligence |
| Using group skills | | Own skills |
| Respect and trust | | Patronise |
| High performance workgroup | | Rigid hierarchy |
| Bottom-up | | Top-down |
| Qualitative measures | | Quantitative measures |

Reprinted with permission from Digital Equipment Corporation (1991).

**Figure 4.1** The nature of leadership

*Good cause*

Your neighbour's two-year-old daughter needs special surgery to cure a rare disease. Funds are needed to send her and her mother abroad to the only hospital able to help. What could you do to help raise funds? Can you think of a service or goods for which people might be willing to pay? How could you persuade other people to help you? How could you organise a fundraising project? Who might help you with advice on running your fundraising effort? Draw up a timetable for the project. Make an estimate of the costs of running such a project.

*Mount an emergency*

Leading a lightweight camping holiday of six people in the Alps, you have all the supplies needed for a week's stay in the mountains. Although it is a summer holiday, the weather has become unsettled with hail and thunderstorms. You have previously left a note of your intended route with a mountain rescue organisation.

On the second night out and six miles from the nearest village you awake to find that John, a member of the party, has rolled out of his tent and fallen from a small ridge. He has injured his ankle and has a nasty bump on his head. Another member of the party suggests that it is John's own fault for pitching his tent in a stupid place. Consider the immediate and long-term problems. Decide together with other members of your camping party the course of action you should take and in what order things should be done. Which of the characteristics of the members of your camping party would be useful in this situation?

### Leadership discussion points

Many business leaders have offered their views on the secrets of their success, but they have not always agreed. Do you agree with any of the opinions expressed?

'Life is based on seeing, listening and experimenting, but experimenting is the most important.'                                                        (Soichiro Honda)

'How did I make my fortune? By always selling too soon. Sell, regret and grow rich.'                                                                   (Nathan Rothschild)

'Don't be conformist. A businessman who wants to be successful cannot afford to imitate others. He must be original, imaginative, resourceful and be an entirely self-reliant entrepreneur.'                                                         (John Paul Getty)

'When you want something from a person, think of what you can give him in return. Let him think it is he who is coming off best.'      (Ernest Oppenheimer)

## PSYCHOMOTOR ABILITY

The development of physical skills to full potential involves a successful interaction between genetic and environmental factors. A knowledge of the former informs our understanding, whilst an appreciation of the latter ensures that we become enablers. Environmental factors are, therefore, the most significant in the promotion of excellence. There is a need for a collaborative strategy between physical education and sport, and physical recreation and health. Physical activity is part of our heritage and psychomotor competence can only enhance the quality of all our lives, as well as allowing us to marvel at the achievements of the gifted athlete. If we believe in a healthy mind and a healthy body, then we need to have a broad view of physical education and sport integrated with other aspects.

Firstly, we need procedural knowledge – in the areas of athletics, dance, games (running games, over-the-net games, striking games, creating games) and swimming, but more is involved than giving enrichment in these different games. There is also knowledge about other parts of the subject to be gained:

• codes of conduct;
• health education;
• first aid;
• information about after-school activities;

- decision making;
- tactics and strategy;
- criticism and analysis;
- rules necessary for safety and hygiene;
- the laws of the sport or game;
- a knowledge of moral, social, aesthetic values.

## Concepts

- The concepts involved in the development of psychomotor ability include:
- awareness of space;
- understanding of effort, such as weight and time;
- technique;
- themes;
- form;
- principles of play;
- adaptability.

## Attitudes

Some of the attitudes that make for a whole person who reaches his/her full potential in the area of psychomotor ability are:

- cooperation;
- courage;
- consideration;
- enthusiasm;
- determination;
- initiative;
- social ability;
- sportsmanship;
- self-motivation;
- supportiveness;
- a sense of humour.

## Skills

The numerous skills to be taught and enhanced in order for children to reach their potential include:

- gymnastics;
- balance skills;
- weight transference skills;
- shape skills;
- flight;
- tactical skills;
- team skills;
- movement skills and body awareness.

This idealistic scheme is very demanding on time and necessitates well-trained specialist teachers. Because of the pressure on the timetable, it is suggested that sports and dance clinics or teach-ins during and outside the school day should be introduced. Home coaching packages could be drawn up and directed by the school, but supported by parents. A continental-style day, with academic time during the morning and compulsory physical education in the afternoon, is to be commended. This should allow for collaboration with outside agencies that can assist with facilities and coaching expertise.

Ideally, every child should have physical education every day, and there should be a progressive system for the development of gymnastic skills, for example, from the pre-school years through to Olympic standard. Teachers should be made aware of the competitive structures available through inter-club, inter-county, regional zone, national and international levels. This structure takes account of relative excellence in competitive gymnastics, for example, as well as giving individual direct access to the top of the tree. This would be an almost impossible task within any one school, but teachers have considerable resources available, including retired performers; teachers and parents should be encouraged to continue in sport, in coaching and in administration. This would enable increased participation by talented children and provide the specialisation to cater for giftedness in any given area of psychomotor ability. A school system, of course, is concerned with the total development of the child and this must include enhancing the considerable psychomotor ability of some children and the availability of sport for all.

In terms of the classroom, there are some difficulties in catering adequately for talented children. There are no 'hard and fast rules' to different types of grouping in PE. It is quite possible that a low-ability group could be keener or better motivated in PE than a group with higher academic ability. What tends to happen, though, is that the brighter students are easier to teach and control because they take information in and are able to act on that information. In general their behaviour, span of concentration and social skills are better than those of less able students. Because safety is of paramount importance, discipline has to be good. A comprehensive school Head of PE writes about some of the difficulties of ability grouping.

> When the whole year group are on together they are divided into equal numbers, done mainly by tutor groupings (as this is the most convenient method). Certain individuals may be kept apart.
>
> Year 7 and Year 11 have some mixed (boys/girls) lessons. We hope to carry this into Year 8 in September 1991.
>
> A few years ago we did try to group into ability: 'A' – the athletic/skilful students; 'B' – the average/well-motivated; 'C' – the poor attenders, badly behaved, less able. This did not work very well as the 'A' group were too arrogant and tended to think they knew it all. The 'C' group numbers were erratic and the ability so poor that progress was difficult. The best group being 'B' – a pleasure to teach.

This academic year we have also had to modify the curriculum, in particular Year 9 girls. They are not interested in 'skill exercises' and in order to get them to bring kit on a regular basis, a more flexible approach is required.

## The integration of minds with physical bodies

In the past, schools have required the physical body to be developed as a separate entity. There is a need to understand energy balance and the problems of stress, to name just two areas. Many forms of relaxation can be used to develop the skill of physically reducing tension. Another area which should be taught through PE is sensory awareness, which is important in expanding the abilities of people. Young children in particular make sense of their environment by using all their senses (see Clarke, 1988, for further information).

When we discuss intelligence, it is important that we do not just think of school activities. The more we understand the human brain, the more we come to realise that intelligence includes our emotional health, our physical ability and health, our creative and intuitive selves, along with our visual and verbal thinking.

## ACADEMIC ABILITY

Much encouragement is given to children in schools as regards their cognitive development, often to the detriment of the other talent areas we are discussing in this chapter. It is generally acknowledged that far too much classroom learning is concerned with traditional academic knowledge and routine skills, rather than teaching children to think, to reason and to solve problems in a creative way. For example, the British National Curriculum is heavily biased towards a knowledge base. It should include concepts, skills and attitude development. Davis and Rimm (1989) suggest there are three basic ways to teach thinking:

(1) strengthening intellectual abilities and skills through practice and exercise;
(2) helping students learn conscious and deliberate strategies for reasoning, problem solving and critical thinking;
(3) increasing students' understanding of their own and others' thinking.

All these involve both inductive reasoning (reaching a conclusion that is somewhat supported) and deductive reasoning (reaching a conclusion that is necessitated by the premises). There is still some debate about when a person is using deductive reasoning or using inductive reasoning. Some philosophers say that the thinker is using whatever kind of reasoning he thinks he is using. Herrmann (1987), speaking at the World Conference on gifted and talented children in Sydney, explained research which has found that some kinds of thinking primarily involve the left hemisphere of the brain, some primarily involve the right hemisphere, whereas other kinds of thinking involve both hemispheres and in particular utilise the *corpus callosum*, which connects the two hemispheres (see George, 1994). For example, pure deductive reasoning, spelling, reading and arithmetic calculations are all left brain. Such things as recognition of patterns, the ability to generalise and, consequently, at least some kinds of inductive reasoning appear to involve primarily the right hemisphere.

It appears to me that most subjects taught in school involve primarily the left hemisphere. If this is the case, then we are giving children an unbalanced curriculum. English, mathematics and science, which are the three core subjects taking most of the time available, are largely left hemisphere subjects, whereas the creative arts, which include perception, fantasy and enjoyment, as well as the ability to see the broad picture, originate in the right hemisphere. Since education seems to concentrate on left-hemisphere thinking activities, this could well be the reason students seldom automatically transfer learning, even within the same subject area, let alone from one subject area to another, or to everyday life situations (for example, relating what the child has done in the science laboratory to solving problems in the world) to either the right hemisphere of the corpus hemisphere or the corpus callosum Drawing reasonable inferences, recognising cause and effect, reasoning by analogy, spatial perception, recognising relations, creativity, and asking and answering such questions as 'what would happen if' involve use of the inductive thinking side of the brain and can be taught and encouraged in children.

Because academic superiority is still perhaps the major reason gifted and talented children are initially identified, then such skills as these should be recognised and encouraged. Of course, it is a matter not just of how well a child is performing in academic subjects, but of a child's approach to a problem and application. For example, Bloom (1985) found that many students engaged in detailed individual activities for long periods of time, asked a lot of questions, learned through observation, enjoyed reading and experimentation, and made use of the knowledge gained. However, this is not always the case. A child may be intellectually superior but poor on application. Gifted is as gifted does. Some of these children can be described as gifted underachievers, and these children often need a great deal of support and counselling, which will be discussed later.

Thinking skills can be strengthened and improved through exercises in the same way as a sports person practises. Creative thinking may be taught directly by helping students to understand creative people and creative processes. Critical thinking may be taught by teaching children to observe and look critically at opinion or a newspaper article. Much of the work of teaching thinking skills has recognised Bloom's impact on this area. His taxonomy (see p. 64) describes progressively higher levels of cognitive activity. At the knowledge and comprehension stages, students deal with definitions, facts and categories, as well as relationships and theories. These are necessary for all students, but gifted and talented students who have a strong knowledge base can move higher up the taxonomy and apply rules and principles, analyse, hypothesise, synthesise and evaluate the accuracy, value and efficiency of an idea or a course of action. These able children can have the earlier part of the taxonomies compacted because they already know a great deal and also learn fast and so can move on to the higher thinking skills.

Children should also be encouraged to think about thinking. This area is commonly called metacognition. Students should understand their thinking strategies, and understand why and when and how these strategies may be used. The de Bono (1973) CORT programmes are prototypes of metacognition in which children are encouraged to function better, not only to be more proficient at solving problems but to enjoy thinking. The CORT thinking skills are taught in a direct metacognitive fashion, whereby children consciously understand the value of each skill and when, why and how it should be applied. There are some 50 CORT thinking skills, of which the following are just some examples:

- challenging existing ways of doing things as a means of stimulating new ideas;
- solving problems by thinking about problem requirements;
- directing something according to their needs and requirements;
- decision making, which requires considering the factors involved, objectives, priorities, consequences and possible alternatives;
- recognising contradictory information which can lead to false conclusions.

The following are a few examples of the type of thinking exercise that teachers and parents should consider teaching their children:

(1) Suppose you were born 100 years from now, how would your life be different from what it is now?
(2) Scientists are gradually finding more cures for different types of cancer. However, it seems that cancer is still killing many more people than it did, say, 50 years ago. Why do you suppose this is?
(3) If you could run your school any way you wanted to, what would you do? Who would you have to teach in it and who would attend your school? Would you have any rules regarding how students should behave in your school? Would you have any rules about school uniform? What would you do about someone who did not obey the rules? Who would pay for the cost of running the school? Would you allow anyone from any age group to attend?
(4) Mary has a blind friend who doesn't know what an elephant is. The friend has heard of an elephant and knows it is an animal, but that is all the friend knows about elephants. How should Mary go about describing an elephant to her friend?
(5) In many parts of the world a lot of deaths are caused by traffic accidents.

It has been estimated that over 50 per cent of fatal accidents involve drivers who have been drinking alcohol. What do you think should be done to reduce the number of fatal accidents?

(6) What would you do if a real UFO landed on the school playing field not far from where you were standing?

(7) On arriving home from school one day, you walk into the kitchen and put the light switch on, but nothing happens. The light does not go on, the light bulb does not flash. What would you do?

See also the Somerset Thinking Skills course, listed in the resources section of Chapter 7.)

## PROVIDING FOR GIFTED AND TALENTED CHILDREN – A SUMMARY

### Considerations

What do we want gifted and talented students to be or do as an outcome of their education?

Is the purpose of education for the gifted and talented to promote the development of self or the contributions they can make to society?

Is learning how to learn more important than what is being learned? Is quantity or quality the focus of a programme?

Should learning emphasise the assimilation of information or the development of thinking processes?

Is the progress of the gifted and talented measured against the group, the average or the self?

Is the winning of prizes, and 'A' grades an indicator of school success?

### Implications

The answers to these questions reflect personal biases, experiences and knowledge. Reviewing the purposes of a programme for the gifted and talented and understanding the elements of a programme can shape values for the programme. What is to be valued for the gifted and talented cannot be separated from research data about the characteristics and needs of these students, contemporary feelings of society about education, and the interests, background and attitudes of the students.

What in-service training is required to increase staff awareness of the needs of these children across the curriculum? A balanced and challenging curriculum which is flexible enough to take account of all children needs to be provided.

### Application

The aims and objectives of an educational programme for the gifted and talented should stress the development of the self as the top priority. Open-ended objectives allow for student determination in the learning process. Student-written aims and objectives are consonant with the concept of self-direction. Goals and objectives which stress the attainment of learning skills such as research, enquiry and problem solving are conducive to teaching students how to learn.

The keeping and monitoring of children's records and profiles is also essential, as is making sure that these children have some power over their own curriculum, which is their entitlement.

## TEACHERS OF THE GIFTED

> A great teacher never strives to explain his vision – he simply invites you to stand beside him and see for yourself.
>
> (Rev. R. Inman)

The teacher has the unique opportunity to make provision for the potentially gifted child to develop and mature so that the child can eventually become a positive and valued member of society. Children, however, also have the right to develop fully as individuals, and it is the right of every child to be child-like. The sympathetic, perceptive, empathising teacher should be aware of some children's lack of synchronisation with their peers, and possibly with their family and their time (see Figure 4.2).

Teachers should understand the feelings of frustration and isolation which can arise when intellectual development surges ahead of emotional and physical development. They will be conscious of the possible disparity between intellectual and social needs – the needs of advanced intellectual development compared with the basic human needs of security and social acceptance. Such teachers need to be sufficiently mature themselves to accept children with high abilities. In addition, teachers need to be humble, accepting the role of being a learner with the child.

Gallagher (1985) identifies three needs of paramount importance: firstly, the need to help talented and gifted children develop study skills; secondly, the need to encourage bright pupils to develop skills of higher-level thinking; and, thirdly, the children's need to be rewarded for scholastic achievement while at the same time retaining an identity with the class group. Note that the emphasis is on the cognitive development of children, whereas we must remember our broader definition and cater for the talent areas that many children have.

Maker (1982b) requires that teachers have:
- a good knowledge of their subjects,
- sympathetic understanding of child development,
- confidence,

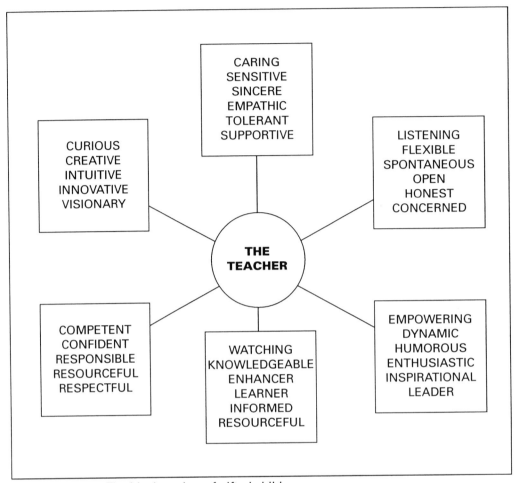

**Figure 4.2**     The ideal teacher of gifted children

- skill in developing flexible and interesting material,
- highly developed skills of questioning and explaining,
- willingness to guide rather than dictate, allowing pupils to develop independence of mind and action,
- proven success as a teacher in the regular classroom,
- an ability to make mistakes.

Undoubtedly one could argue that all children would benefit from contact with teachers possessing these qualities. Teachers, and especially head teachers, need the qualities of leadership – one of the talent areas that some children have.

It surprises me that we do not ask children nearly often enough what they would like to learn, what their ideal classroom would be like, how they could solve some of the problems of the school, and to give examples. Endean and George (1982) asked nine ten-year-old gifted children what they thought the ideal teacher should be like and their responses represent quite a challenge to any teacher.

## The ideal science teacher

Almost all required that the teacher be master of his subject. Some (girls) specified that the teacher was to be well educated in all areas, not just in science. Almost as universally prescribed was a sense of humour. It was felt this was conducive to an easy but not slack atmosphere in the classroom, and it was mentioned that it helped to make the lesson fun and so motivated them to learn. The paragon is also required to be a good communicator. He must be able to convey the essence of difficult new concepts in a readily understood and simple manner. The importance of his using 'everyday language' and being able to give 'everyday examples' was stressed. One respondent added that if there were not an everyday application to hand, then the teacher should be able to supply a good analogy.

A group of respondents (girls) placed considerable emphasis on the teacher explaining individual errors to students, so that they could understand their own mistakes and avoid making the same errors in future. Several (mainly boys) prescribed a teacher who felt personally involved with the pupils and with the work they produced. An equally sized group (mainly girls) stressed the importance of the teacher being able to inspire zest and having the power to motivate them to learn.

Generally, the ideal teacher should set up and maintain a well-structured but informal learning environment within which pupils could suggest their own ideas and experiments (this from the girls), discuss ideas and errors, and, owing to his consummate pedagogical skills, all could progress at their own individual rate without hold-ups.

On another occasion I asked a group of nine-year-old children at a summer school what they expected from a teacher. Their responses were: discipline; sense of humour; caring; sympathy when in difficulty; ability to explain problems; encouragement to look forward to lessons; no favourites; good appearance; variety in lessons; learning made easy; understanding of pupils' viewpoint. Some researchers would have taken considerable time to come up with this list!

In the light of the above, perhaps we should ask ourselves the following questions :

- What am I doing to encourage and develop interest shown by individual children?
- How far are the children learning independently?

- What attitudes are the more able children developing towards their own ability, and am I acting as a positive counsellor and enhancer?
- Are the children positively involved by their attitudes towards their less able peers?
- What opportunity do these children have to work with a group of like-minded children of similar ability?

## Head teachers

Head teachers can make things happen in their school. They are responsible for school policy, whether it be for special needs children, the needs of our multi-cultural society, equal opportunities, the new technologies, the home and environment, or the children we are discussing here. It is because of the power of head teachers in the school system that I pause and consider what qualities of leadership we should expect from head teachers. They are not just managers of resources. Good head teachers stand out by being different, they question assumptions and are suspicious of traditions. They make decisions based on fact and not on prejudice and have a preference for innovation. Such leaders are observant and sensitive to people, they know their team well, they have a talented pool of staff and develop mutual confidence within their team.

Head teachers should state clear objectives and encourage a sense of security by defining territory for individual action. They should delegate real authority and not interfere unless it is necessary. They should praise more often than they criticise. Maslow's (1954) hierarchy of human needs is for all mankind, not just for gifted and talented children (as we shall discuss in Chapter 6).

If we can select and educate head teachers with these characteristics, then teachers, who have an exhausting job to do, will follow them with respect and even with affection and a sense of curiosity, because they make life enjoyable for the team by the promise of surprise, excitement but, above all, solid achievement for all children. If good teachers are the most valuable resource in creating opportunities for gifted and talented children, time is the second most valuable resource. Of course, teachers and time are both costly. There is no escaping the fact that it takes time to maintain a highly trained professional teaching force, and, because I believe that children are the most precious resource that we possess, both time and money should be found for them.

## Courses for teachers

In initial teacher training, there is insufficient time to do justice to the many areas that students today need to cover in order to be confident and competent teachers in the classroom. There are obviously competing pressures coupled with the varying concerns of staff, and it is not easy to make a case for a substantial part of any teacher training course to cover the area of gifted education. This is probably best left to near the end of a Bachelor of Education degree course when students can capitalise upon the knowledge, skills and experience acquired earlier in the course. In initial teacher training, students should be trained to be aware of the most able children and to understand the needs of all children and how they should be educated as whole people. It is appropriate to deal with the issue in the general context of catering for individual differences, rather than as a totally separate issue. Thus, general matters arising in connection with child development, learning strategies and individual differences have to be considered first, followed by concentration on the education of both less able and the more able as exemplars of similarities and differences in need and strategies in provision.

Once a teacher has been teaching for a while in school, then is the time to build on that essential experience to study the needs of the most able children in greater depth through in-service courses and higher degrees.

## THE ORGANISATION OF PROVISION

### Teaching strategies

The implementation of appropriate and specific strategies in the regular classroom will form a solid basis for the education of gifted and talented students, and some of these issues have already been discussed.

**Figure 4.3** The organisation of provision

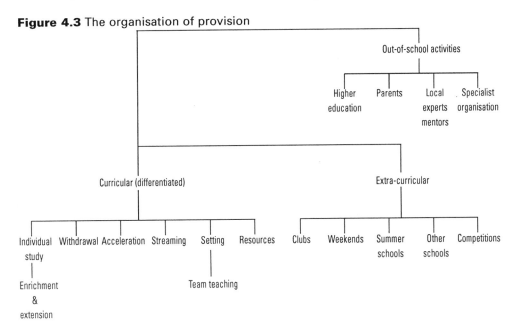

Grouping is the provision of various organisational structures of either long or short duration, whereby students of a like ability can work together. One of these categories is full-time homogeneous grouping, such as the magnet schools in the USA, where students of various ability levels are taken to the particular school that accommodates their needs and career interests. Another category is commonly called cluster grouping and involves placing a group of gifted students in the same regular class for special assignments and field trips. This could mean that the regular common core curriculum may be compacted to allow time for enrichment activities.

In some countries, of course, there are special schools for the gifted, as in America and Israel. In the UK there are the famous choir schools, the Royal Ballet School and the Yehudi Menuhin School of Music, to name but a few. On the whole, however, segregating children is not favoured ideologically.

Indeed, for the same reasons, teaching in the UK has tended to be in mixed-ability groups. Here the teacher has to be an excellent manager and disciplinarian in order to make sure that children reach the higher potential of which they are capable. Mixed-ability grouping was, in part, a reaction to the rigid banding and streaming that existed in most UK schools.

Streaming is an organisational method that is in danger of hinging around quantity rather than trying to create qualitatively different work. It is based on the theory that pupils who are of a certain ability in one area are therefore of similar ability in most areas. This is an outdated and disproven theory.

Setting, while being an improvement, has many drawbacks, as well as some benefits. Primary school teachers in England seem to provide work of a more advanced nature to the top set in any one class, which should be appropriate to meeting the needs of the intellectual characteristics mentioned earlier. However, the work carried out in sets or bands is usually too rigid, too structured and lacking in the open-ended problem-solving elements needed to allow the potential of highly able children to flourish.

A process-centred approach is an alternative to adopt with very able children. If we can identify the higher-level intellectual abilities and talents, then they can form the basis of any enrichment or extension work with very able children. Organisationally, such work could be designed to fit into normal school lessons, with the most able working on this kind of material in the same classroom as the rest of the class, who will proceed with their usual work. Alternatively, the most able could be withdrawn, as in remedial education, to attend some process-centred sessions. This imaginative and stimulating approach tries to provide some qualitatively different work for the very able. We must remember, however, that it is not just the very able who are capable of using these higher-level intellectual skills; process-centred work should form part of the curriculum for every child. The other concern is that much of the package material available for very able children is still teacher directed, is lacking in the provision of opportunities for open-ended problem solving and investigation, and is all too often carried out in much the same way as other school work.

Experience has shown that students of similar ability levels work well together despite age differences, and the scheduling of some class time should be allowed for this type of activity. The time may be used for tutorial work, with the older student instructing or leading the younger intellectual peer. Projects should be cooperative in nature, with students of different grades who have similar interests or strengths being grouped to pursue a selected topic. Such a grouping would allow for the efficient use of the resources necessary.

## Mentorship

Teachers should be humble enough to realise that it is not always possible to extend gifted and talented children to the full and that there are many people in the community who would be delighted to help in various ways. For example, a student could be matched up with a person who has been made redundant who has a similar enthusiasm and ability for a certain topic or subject. These community resources are available and, where curriculum compacting has been achieved, this mentorship model can provide a very worthwhile learning experience for able children. A typical scenario will be where an adult member of the community and a single student meet regularly over a period of months, with the student possibly visiting the mentor at the job site to learn, first hand and in detail, the activities, responsibilities, problems and lifestyle associated with a particular business, profession or art. Of course, mentorship presumes a commitment on the part of the student and the mentor to plan a detailed sequence of learning activities designed to achieve a specified goal.

## Counselling

Some of the children we have been discussing, and their parents too, would benefit from counselling. It would provide a support system for gifted and talented students and pay attention to their social and emotional well-being, as well as their academic needs. Every effort should be made to improve the well-being of students by providing help with normal developmental tasks, as well as with the special problems associated with being gifted. One obvious problem is dealing with expectations, because some of these students find the level of achievement which they should be attaining in conflict with the expectations of their parents and teachers. For example, some girls continue to have difficulty in making decisions about taking courses in non-traditional career areas, such as mathematics. Students could also be helped with the skills involved in studying and the management of time.

One challenge to any school is to identify the talent pool of staff, because teachers have hidden interests just like the children. Other areas within a school where counselling could take place would be in small tutorial groups, or for a few minutes at lunchtime or after school with a teacher who has a similar interest to that of the gifted child.

Ideally, each school should have a counsellor, who would be part of the school team, consulting the classroom teachers, and encouraging the use of peer group dynamics to reinforce student cooperation. This occurs in most schools in the area of career counselling and this should start early, because gifted children need assistance in defining career goals and identifying appropriate routes early in their school careers. Counselling is an important element in any gifted education programme, but staffing levels in British schools are not usually good enough to cope. It is hoped that, one day, there will be a counsellor appointed at least to every secondary school, as happens in North America.

The tutorial system in British schools is a sporadic one and requires a coherent plan, because many gifted and talented children need support. They may have personal and social concerns, as well as educational and careers decisions to make. Parents and teachers can support one another here to help their children discover interests and abilities and to relate these to lifestyle, educational and career opportunities. There is often a need for family counselling, because some parents are bewildered, disbelieving, fearful, or even resentful of their child's abilities. The NAGC Counselling Service is recommended to both parents and schools.

Career development is one of the few areas of provision that is supported by research (Shore, 1991). Career counselling helps children to mark career possibilities early and should favour open-ended choices that allow for further challenge and growth. This is vital for the broadly gifted child who is good at everything and yet, having gained 10 'A' grades at GCSE, has to make a decision about 'A' levels.

Some parents put considerable pressure on their children to follow in the family business, or to go into a career that does not coincide with their child's true desire. Girls in particular may need convincing that career and family are compatible, and children from poor backgrounds and some ethnic groups may need their sights setting higher. Professional models from similar disadvantaged backgrounds can be a vital component of a successful career service.

### Extra-mural activities

In most countries there are special summer schools and Saturday classes where courses of study are provided in one or more areas for gifted and talented students. The students are able to pursue knowledge and skills with other students of superior ability, and this has been shown to be a stimulating experience for them. Many colleges and universities, with their staff of experts, would be delighted to help a child or group of children who have a fascination for a particular subject (Endean and George, 1982).

### Using the library more efficiently

It is essential to ensure that students receive their full entitlement to books and literature. Someone has wisely said that 'a blessed companion is a book'. It is the work of everyone in education, and not just teachers, to shape and be inspired by strong and sound values and to give pupils a chance of acquiring and, it is to be hoped, living by those values. In these days of economic stringency, this, in a very vital sense, would give the country value for money, because an investment in values will provide just the kind of return that is needed.

HMI, Trevor Dickinson, at a conference in 1989, stressed that it is important to see the National Curriculum as a framework, and to build for children a rich educational experience around it. In particular, he stressed that literature offers joy, creativity, and the chance for children to see as others see, to feel as others feel and to move beyond narrow confines of space and time. Literature also demands that readers ask vital questions about life and living and, in this sense, literature and poetry are important prompts to thought. They are also powerful aids to growth and language confidence. However, it is a question not just of the availability of good literature, but of the use the children make of good literature, including reference material in the library. There are skills to be taught here so that children can research a project on their own and be aware of literature retrieval methodologies .

## COMPUTER TECHNOLOGY

Computer technology is an educational resource whose potential still is largely unexploited within schools, despite the best efforts of government to put computers into schools and the intense marketing of a wide range of educational products by computer-related suppliers. This lack is, in part, due to the very high rate of technical change – as soon as a teacher begins to gain confidence with one programme it is superseded by another which offers much more but is yet more complex. The key role of information technology has been fully recognised within the National Curriculum, as have the ways in which computers can engage and excite children and enrich their learning.

**The National Curriculum:**

In primary schools within Key Stages 1 and 2 it is expected that computers will be used naturally within the curriculum, using simple packages (art, DTP, spreadsheets, databases), CD-roms, and possibly the Internet. In many schools pupils are regularly engaged in finding information from CD-rom encyclopaedias such as *Encarta* to use within projects. They can be found using simple desktop publishing packages to produce class magazines or school newspapers. Their range of artwork is often enhanced by using painting or graphics packages. They can also do class surveys, feed the results into a simple database and then analyse their results. In a growing number of primary schools, e-mail on the Internet is being used as a means of linking schools and pupils together in the global community. In the very near future primary schools will be involved in video links around the world, as already happens in the USA.

At Key Stage 3 in secondary schools it is expected that children will learn the range of skills needed for using full-scale databases, spreadsheets and word-processors. Besides these skills, they are expected to be introduced to computing as it applies to every subject. Thus in English they might use word-processing for presentation of their work or DTP for media. In CDT they might learn to use computer-aided design (CAD) to assist project work or control programmes to operate power-articulated models. In science their experimental readings can be fed directly into a computer and accurate graphs produced. In music they can use synthesisers and MIDI to compose their own electronic music. History and geography are well served by databases on CD-rom or the Internet. Pupils are also expected to learn about the social implications of computers and how they will affect their lives.

At Key Stage 4 and beyond students are expected to use the full range of computer applications for individual use in support of their curriculum studies. Teachers are expected to be able to enrich their teaching by using a wide range of teaching strategies, including the creative application of computing techniques. The National Curriculum makes heavy demands on teachers' IT skills and expects them to raise these significantly.

## Individualised learning

Working on a computer is a solitary rather than a group activity and in this respect it is ideal for individualised learning of many forms. There have been many educational experiments in the past which have shown that pupils are highly motivated when able to take control of their learning. Computers are highly flexible devices which can instantly change from being an aid to writing into a database of historical or physical facts, from a design tool into a calculator, or from a scientific counter into a full sound and colour multi-media presentation. There are clear opportunities for able pupils to extend their learning experiences and for teachers to manage effective curriculum differentiation. There is evidence that, by individualising the curriculum, able children will achieve higher, undertake more collateral reading and use more school resources, and there will be fewer discipline problems.

## The future – the Information Superhighway

The rate of change of technology is so great that it is impossible to predict what may be in the very near future. The Information Superhighway is, however, certain to come and to have a major influence on the way in which schools provide educational experiences. Many schools are already subscribers to the Internet, and the Information Superhighway is an extension of this. It will provide much more information, however, in the forms of higher speeds of access, full sound and full video. Unlike many revolutions in education, the Information Revolution is being driven by factors outside schools – the cable companies, the telecommunications companies and the satellite broadcasters. The one fact we can be sure of is that able children will be far more at home with this new technology, its methods and its flexibility than anyone in the generations seeking to induct them into the world of knowledge and wisdom!

## Contacts with the local community

Many organisations, such as the Royal Society for the Protection of Birds or the local history society, have junior membership and this can be a good outlet for students whose enthusiasm and abilities exceed the regularly offered course work.

Saturday schools and summer camps are increasingly popular and have the advantage of permitting gifted children to meet like-minded children away from the restrictions of a busy school life. Most Saturday schools are run by NAGC in Britain, or by a higher education institution, and are taught by volunteer specialist teachers, lecturers or community experts, assisted by the parents of the gifted child. Normally the children attending are selected by teachers as being able to benefit from being extended and the programmes are designed to be inclusive and not exclusive (Endean and George, 1982; Davis and Rimm, 1989).

Children with a mentor from the local community can learn a great deal about the lifestyle of mentors and the problems of industry, commerce and the professions, as well as the mentor acting as a role model. It is important carefully to match the mentor to the child, to have a clear plan of objectives and to evaluate progress. Ideally, double mentoring is recommended, whereby a mentor from the community is shadowed by a professional teacher to ensure development is progressive. This may involve regular in-school and after-

**Figure 4.4**

---

### Community Resource Survey
### To Parents and Friends of the School

We now have a policy in the school for supporting our most able children and are looking for volunteers to share their knowledge and experience with our children. We are aware that our community is represented by many professions, trades, vocations, as well as hobbies and interests. If you are willing to support us in this way, then we would appreciate it if you would complete this form and return it to the school as soon as possible.

Name ................................................................Address ........................................................

Occupation ...............................................................................................................................

Business Tel. No ...............................................Home Tel. No ...........................................

Below are areas which could supplement the curriculum for your children and help to extend them in order to help them reach their full potential. Please complete the form by indicating what you could offer, e.g. talk, practical demonstration, written materials, visual aids or displays:

*Sciences:*
Biology
Conservation
Geology
Chemistry
Astronomy
etc.

*Social Sciences:*
Travel
Geography
History
Economics
Sociology
etc.

*Professions/Trades:*
Doctor
Para-medic
Nursing
Law
Vet
Plumber
Policeman
Engineer
etc.

*General:*
Arts, Crafts
Music
Literature
Business
Languages
Social Work
Journalism
Insurance
etc.

*Hobbies:*
Photography
Stamps
Music
Painting
Fishing
Gardening
Model Making
Horses
etc.

school meetings. Because teaching is too demanding to allow schools to do everything themselves, the talent pool of the community is a vital resource. The school coordinator for gifted and talented children should seek out members of the community from all walks of life, who are willing to share not only their expertise with children, but also time, patience and understanding. A suggested approach to the community for support in this area is shown on Figure 4.4.

A further aid to motivate these children is to provide them with a contract worksheet each week. A typical recommended example is shown in Figure 4.5.

## Acceleration

Any teaching strategy that results in placement beyond a child's chronological age is titled acceleration and this is the most popular way of coping with more able children in Britain (NAGC, 1990a; Shore, 1991). The 1988 Education Reform Act assumes that most children will reach attainment targets 6 or 7, but also that some will reach 9 or 10. It thus recognises able children who may reach this level. However, there is little cognisance of the wide range of abilities found in any one class of children, or of their different needs; the curriculum content is the same for all.

The subject has been studied extensively and research has supported the use of acceleration with more able children (Gold, 1979). Brody and Benbow (1987) noted that acceleration offers students the opportunity to select a programme of work that is both challenging and interesting. It is also helpful to the school because it does not have to develop and implement a special programme for such children. Acceleration should, however, mean accelerated learning within the classroom, not just missing a year. It can mean early entry at all stages but especially telescoping or compacting the curriculum to give time for challenging and different work, thus improving motivation, preventing laziness and underachievement, as well as reducing arrogance in some children. Compaction means eliminating tasks that are repetitious, reproductive and regurgitive. Able children should certainly have the opportunity to work at their own rapid pace, to progress through and out of primary school into the secondary phase and beyond. Acceleration that speeds up learning time to match students' potential and capabilities is to be welcomed.

Early admission to infant school should involve careful screening. Such children should be intellectually precocious, reasonable at motor coordination, have good health and social maturity and possess adequate reading skills. Early admission to the junior and secondary phases of education will benefit children who are ready for a more specialised course, but it will probably mean abandoning friends.

There are, however, critics of this approach and they warn of its potential

**Figure 4.5**

# Contract Worksheet

The following is an example of a basic contract form on which pupils clarify tasks to be completed within a self-organised time-frame. A series of questions guide them in the assessment of their work behaviours.

<u>PUPIL TASK SHEET</u>

| Date/time | *Task to be worked on*<br>(state clearly *what* you intend<br>to do and *when*) | Checklist/work due<br>(list ongoing tasks and<br>when they are due) |
| --- | --- | --- |

| EVALUATION – How well did you work? | M | T | W | T | F |
| --- | --- | --- | --- | --- | --- |
| 1. I moved quietly and settled to my tasks quickly | | | | | |
| 2. I listened carefully and followed the instructions | | | | | |
| 3. I worked quietly not disturbing others | | | | | |
| 4. I planned and organised my time well | | | | | |
| 5. I used my spare time wisely | | | | | |
| 6. I completed my tasks giving thought and effort | | | | | |
| 7. I participated in discussion groups | | | | | |
| 8. I proof-read and checked my work before handing in | | | | | |
| 9. I corrected any errors and added words to my learning list | | | | | |
| 10. I thought about neat handwriting/presentation | | | | | |
| 11. I worked well unsupervised | | | | | |
| 12. I handed in and collected my work daily | | | | | |

problems. Coleman (1985) suggests that acceleration results in teaching the same material, only teaching it faster. He also suggests that it can lead to emotional and social maladjustment.

The majority of the literature does not support this latter point (Whitmore, 1981; Birch et al., 1965); nevertheless, the choice of acceleration is a crucial decision. Teachers and parents are referred to the checklist below, which should be carefully considered before accelerating a child, a step that may be irreversible. For example, not all children progress steadily through their school career and, if a child's development slows, it could cause feelings of failure and frustration. Perhaps most important of all are the differing rates of a child's emotional and social development in relation to academic growth. Having left friends behind, a child could find him/herself in an atmosphere that is not conducive to personal growth and development. This could lead to difficulties in the ability to make good social relationships and to consequent long-term unhappiness. The risk can be considerably tempered when acceleration is modified to part-time attendance in a higher class for a child's specific talent area. Examples of this practice are Johns Hopkins University in the USA and the Royal Institution maths and science master classes in London and elsewhere. Vernon (1977) offers evidence that adverse effects can be minimised when the following criteria are carefully judged for each child.

- the child is adequately prepared psychologically,
- the teachers of the new classes are sensitive and aware,
- the child is both emotionally and physically mature,
- the child is not accelerated more than one year,
- the child really is capable of advanced work.

By allowing a very able child to jump some of the normal school curriculum by moving into an older class, it is hoped that the child will be more stimulated, be less bored and enjoy school better. It is also the easiest administrative way out of the problem. Above all, it should be emphasised that all programmes must be designed to produce sensible, defensible and valuable educational goals.

*Checklist of criteria to be met for consideration of early promotion*

to be used more as a safeguard than rigidly.

- attainments well above average for age;
- evidence of exceptional ability from tests and performance;
- emotional and social maturity for age;
- can cope with physical activities with reasonable motor coordination;
- anxiety and perseverance at reasonable level without evidence of stress or obsessional behaviour;

- parental agreement and support;
- school agreement and support;
- readiness of child to separate from friendship group. Are older friends already established?

*Factors to be borne in mind:*

(1)  A decision made at eight years old can rarely be changed later – repeating a year later on is bad for morale.
(2)  The child may be functioning five years in advance, not just one – marginal benefit?
(3)  There may be an impact on other children in the family.
(4)  Early promotion affects classroom organisation and policy in the school, e.g. all age groups, large ranges of ability.

*The benefits of a 'second opinion'* (e.g. school educational psychologist)

- to confirm that the child has exceptional abilities unlike others in the peer group and that this has been consistent;
- to confirm that the child has the necessary emotional maturity;
- to confirm that the social integration is likely to be successful;
- to consider the long-term consequences;
- to protect the child from an over-ambitious parent or teacher;
- to check that the child is not being used to fulfil the needs of an adult;
- to protect the teachers from parental pressure and ill-will;
- to give parents access to professional advice that can continue when the child has left the present school.

## POINTS FOR DISCUSSION

(1)  What important differences are there between the highly gifted child and a 'great' man or woman?
(2)  In what sense can we say that the difference between a highly gifted child and a bright, able child is as great as or greater than the difference between that bright, able child and a child of average abilities?
(3)  Why does the meeting of the needs of a gifted or talented child in terms of equality of opportunity mean unequal treatment?
(4)  Is this additional and/or different treatment ethically sound when all that could be done is not being done for children with 'negative' rather than 'positive' handicaps?
(5)  How can general class teachers, who are often outstripped in intellect and skills by gifted and talented youngsters, best cope with them and with their own inadequacies?
(6)  Elitist intellectual groups seem ruled out by British social philosophy; is

there a place in the UK for specialist schools to encourage a particular talent, for example art, ballet, music, along with a general education (as, for example, in Russia, Israel and, to a lesser extent, the UK?) There are, after all, a few specialist schools in the UK and, indeed, children have been extracted for special activities for some time – for example, for music, for which there are peripatetic specialists, and for games.

(7)   If the answer to (6) is 'Yes', then what about science and maths? And then where do you draw the line?

   See also the published school policy of King's School, Ottery St Mary, Devon, and George (1995).

## PROGRAMME EVALUATION

An evaluation of programmes for the gifted and talented should be based on the areas and objectives of the programme and be diagnostic. Various points of view should be sought from the children, parents, teachers and management of the school. The evaluation scheme should be on-going and thereby allow quick reaction to faults and strengths. This will enable planning, development and accountability from a natural sequence of educational objectives. It must be recognised that the evaluation of these programmes requires awareness of the problems associated with assessing higher-level objectives, the unsuitability of conventional standardised tests and the practical demands on time, money and trained personnel. The evaluation could take the form of pre and post tests, and teacher, parent and children questionnaires. Above all, ask the children; they have so much to contribute (Endean and George, 1982).

# CHAPTER 5

# Enriching the Curriculum

> Do not believe in a fate that falls on men however they act; but I do believe in a fate that falls on men unless they act.
> (G. K. Chesterton)

> They are able because they think they are able.
> (Virgil)

> It's not my gratitude but my attitude that will determine my attitude.
> (Jesse Jackson)

There are many variations in the interpretation of the term 'enrichment', although most people find common ground in the inclusion of a number of ideas. This was recognised by Ogilvie (1973) when he stated that '"enrichment" will mean different things to different people, and represents something of an amalgam in the minds of us all'. It is defined in the DES glossary as: 'General term for a change in quality of work to a level much higher than that normally expected of a particular age group. Enrichment materials purport to promote or support a higher level of thinking' (DES, 1986).

> Those who teach mathematics must take into account the great variation which exists between pupils both in their rate of learning and also in their level of attainment at any age. It follows that mathematics courses must be matched both in level and pace to the needs of pupils; and therefore, a 'differentiated curriculum' must be provided so that pupils will be enabled to develop to the full their mathematical skill and understanding, a positive attitude towards mathematics, and confidence in making use of it.
> (Cockcroft, 1982)

Reports from many sources have commented upon the disturbing evidence relating to able children and the work which they are asked to do. The following extracts illustrate the point:

> In almost all the cases where work was not reasonably matched to children's capabilities, it was insufficiently demanding. It was very rare for children in any age or ability group to be required to undertake work which was too difficult for them.
> (DES, 1978)

> In a large minority of cases, teachers' expectations of what pupils could achieve are clouded by inadequate knowledge and understanding of each pupil's aptitudes and difficulties; teaching is frequently directed at the middle level of ability so that the most able pupils are understretched and the least able cannot cope. (DES, 1985b)

This particular comment concerned secondary schools.

> There is, however, a good deal of evidence from the survey to suggest that more

able pupils need more opportunities and stimulus to pursue their own initiatives.                                                       (DES, 1985b, Ch. 6)

The definition accepted by the Oxford Research Project (1985), to which I contributed, is that enrichment

(1)   Is a broadening and deepening of the learning experience.
(2)   Provides experiences and activities beyond the regular curriculum.
(3)   Develops the intellectual gifts and talents of the most able.
(4)   Stresses qualitative development of thinking skills rather than quantitative accumulation of facts.
(5)   Emphasises the process of learning rather than content.
(6)   Can be horizontal, exploring bodies of knowledge that are not frequently touched upon in the school common core curriculum.
(7)   Can be vertical, developing the skill of quantitative thinking which implies a facility with subject matter and ability to understand basic principles and to make generalisations.
(8)   Generally involves children doing less and learning more. For example, it is generally preferable for a pupil to find three possible solutions to a problem than to solve three problems of a similar nature.

## CURRICULUM FOR THE GIFTED AND TALENTED

All enrichment activities should be planned and designed with the following objectives in mind (Davis and Rimm, 1989):

• maximum achievement in basic skills
• content beyond the National Curriculum
• exposure to a variety of fields of study
• student-selected content
• high content complexity
• creative thinking and problem solving
• development of thinking skills
• attentive development
• motivation

It seems logical to consider enrichment and differentiated work together, because the concept of enrichment leads directly to differentiated work. Most teachers provide a measure of enrichment work by writing suitable worksheets, modifying text and encouraging children to read widely. As seen above, however, the process of enrichment is more than a simple provision of more demanding materials. Enrichment is a function of the teacher's flexibility, sensitivity and individual needs, a sense of timing and a mastery of subject area.

Planned interaction with other able pupils should be a part of any individual's enrichment programme, and teachers should consciously direct the study programme of each individual pupil so that they know when to enter into a dialogue with the pupil and when to inject new material of suitable variety.

As we have seen above, enrichment and extension of all pupils is important. There is often a mismatch between the work that is given to able pupils and what they are capable of doing. An observant teacher will note that some children cope easily with the work set and will need to make greater demands so that interest and enthusiasm are not lost. Butler-Por (1987), in her excellent book on underachievers, quotes the following poem, which is a sad indictment of some teachers:

> 'To Learn the Bible'
> Today I am so happy
> Today I am going to learn
> How the world was created.
> How the world was chaos,
> And by God's hand changed.
> I shall start to study diligently,
> I shall be an industrious pupil.
> Now I am so happy –
> I shall learn how things began

Three weeks later, Inbal wrote in her diary:

> To learn the Bible is awful,
> All the time to listen
> All the time to write and hear
> A story I think did not happen.
> O how terrible to learn everything by heart.
> To read it to the teacher, nicely.
> I wish the Bible will not be taught –
> For each story to be repeated twice!

Here we have a naturally curious child who had a need to discover and understand. This is a strong intrinsic, motivational force in any child's learning. Inbal had encouraging, urging and fulfilling experiences at home, and hoped this would continue at school, but the teacher succeeded in killing her initial curiosity in an area of learning that held so much promise for this child of seven. It is to be hoped that some future teacher will rekindle her interest and enthusiasm.

The Collins dictionary (1986) defines enrichment as to 'increase the wealth of, to endow with fine or desirable qualities, to enrich one's experience, improve in quality, to enhance, to make more productive'. Enrichment, then, can be any type of activity outside the core of learning that most pupils undertake. Eyre and Marjoram (1990) state:

> enrichment is a process by which school work becomes alive and exciting, and by

which learning is an organic, growing, never-ending, but ever-fascinating journey. It is not about perfunctory completion of routine tasks, but about enlarging horizons, tackling problems whose solutions give rise to further problems, seeking peaks, experimenting with new materials, processes and ideas. It is also about enhancing the quality of life in the classroom and heightening sensitivity.

This philosophical and idealistic statement challenges all teachers to consider how they match up in what they provide for their children. Here are some of the questions all teachers should ask themselves:

(1) To what extent is the work we give our children individualised and designed for the more able of a group?
(2) Do our worksheets allow for variations in the quality of thinking, or do gifted children merely finish more quickly than the rest of the class?
(3) What techniques do we use to set differentiated work? Do we set differentiated tasks? Do the tasks really present new challenges, or just 'more of the same'?
(4) To what extent do we use whole class methods and how do they challenge the gifted child?
(5) Are potential developments of a topic adequately resourced? Teachers all complain about the lack of resources, but they are the most important, expensive resource of any school and perhaps they should also consider what is already available in their school by looking at their stockbooks and seeing what equipment has been accumulated over the years.
(6) How often do we offer suggestions for further reading that utilises vocabulary or concepts well above the levels used in whole class teaching?
(7) Do we promote a policy of differentiated homework? Is this desirable? Homework is possibly the best example of individualisation of the curriculum we have available to us. It should be standard practice for sets to be given differentiated homework, but is there need for more careful differentiation?

These are challenging times, and these are challenging questions. With teacher appraisal, teachers should at least ask themselves these questions, and others, if they are to live up to the status of true professionalism. Basic questions should be asked at the end of every day by every teacher. What have I done today? What have the children done today? What have the children learnt today? What have I learnt today? How have the children and I spent our time? How many questions did we allow the children to ask today? The Collins dictionary gives a definition of extension as 'to draw out, or to be drawn out, to broaden the scope or meaning, to widen, to stretch or expand'. This implies that children move through the curriculum at a different pace in a process of moving to a higher level of skill or to a more difficult concept. The two terms 'extension' and 'enrichment' seem to overlap and they are often used interchangeably and synonymously, but should not be seen as the same thing. They have different aims and functions in the classroom, with enrichment meaning to broaden the horizons and experience of children and extension meaning to move children to higher-order skills, concepts and attitudes.

The National Curriculum emphasises that the curriculum for all children should have breadth and depth, as well as balance and relevance, and all this cannot be provided by the National Curriculum alone. The National Curriculum is a foundation to be augmented by additional subjects, cross-curricular themes, dimensions and skills and extra-curricular activities. The vision for the more able child must be made within this framework. Descriptions of school subjects embodied in legislation are not intended to be exhaustive, and enrichment programmes must draw on a broader conceptualisation of the subjects. For example, the technology order has little content as such, but gives children and teachers the opportunity to develop their own ideas. Primary pupils will have the opportunity to work uninterrupted for a day or two on activities that have a focus on design in technology, whereas in secondary schools design and technology activities will typically extend over half a term. It is essential that careful consideration be given to both the whole curriculum and the individual subject curriculum for the able child. For pupils with an uneven profile across attainment levels, can breadth be sacrificed for part of a key stage to allow for specialisation in certain attainment targets, provided a scheme of work across the key stage as a whole is balanced? Although it is permissible to move pupils up or down a key stage, groups or schools may be exempted from part or all of National Curriculum requirements. However, this is not necessary because the key stage is defined by the average of the group. The value of moving pupils needs careful consideration. Such pupils might gain more by remaining with their peers and being given the benefit of a broader range of learning context, innovative teaching methods and greater flexibility in learning approaches. This should include the use of self-supported study in the same subject, but where the material is broader than that suggested in the attainment targets specified by law. Extended work experience may be of enormous benefit to older pupils, as would the provision of tasks that address real problems and issues.

The National Association for Able Children in Education has published a number of individual learning kits which will enable a gifted child, on occasions, to work on their own, at their own pace, and to be semi-independent of a busy teacher. These materials provide genuine enrichment over and above the National Curriculum materials and enable children to go as far and as fast as they can without any brakes being put on them.

Where pupils do work outside their key stage, careful consideration has to be given to the age appropriateness of schemes of work – the level of maturity of the pupil, on the one hand, and the curriculum content on the other, may be mismatched. If a decision is taken for a pupil to work in the next key stage, it may be difficult to find programmes of study at the right level in all subjects. Whereas, in mathematics, for example, programmes of study are level related, in science they are key stage related. These are essential subjects for gifted and talented children.

If a pupil is to work for most of the time on programmes of study from the next key stage and remain in his or her peer group, disapplication will be required. However, when would the decision be made to disapply? Take Key Stages 3 and 4 for example; if the level of achievement for a subject is not to be assigned to a pupil until the end of the key stage, the teacher could make provision for the next key stage without disapplication from the range of levels, while keeping the pupil in his or her peer group. However, there will be some pupils who might – in mathematics for example – achieve levels 7 or 8 by the end of Key Stage 2; they would start Key Stage 3 only just within the range of levels 3-8, and would, therefore, have every expectation of starting Key Stage 4 work before the end of Key Stage 3. Disapplication from the Key Stage 3 range of levels in this case would seem likely if the pupil was to continue working with Key Stage 3 peers.

The National Curriculum Council once expressed the view that the option of Special Educational Needs pupils working with younger pupils in an earlier key stage would not often be practicable or desirable. Does the same argument hold for pupils working with older pupils from the next key stage? An alternative may be withdrawal of exceptionally able pupils for individual provision for part of the week.

The legislation takes into account the special circumstances of vertically grouped primary classes where the head teacher can assign pupils to a key stage according to an individual's age, rather than according to the age of the majority in the class. This facility in primary schools does not, however, facilitate accelerated progression, where this is deemed appropriate, without, apparently, the need for disapplication because of adherence to designation of key stage by age rather than by levels of achievement. This aspect of the legislation may impede consideration of pupil-groupings that are other than age related.

It is likely that enrichment programmes associated with each attainment level will be developed from amplification, elaboration and extension of the programmes of study at the same level of attainment rather than the next level of attainment (see Figure 5.1). Enrichment programmes of various kinds should benefit all pupils from the most to the least able. Additions to the core must be both interesting and challenging or some pupils will make the core activities fill the time available.

| LEAST | ALL | ABOVE | MOST |
| ABLE | PUPILS | AVERAGE | ABLE |

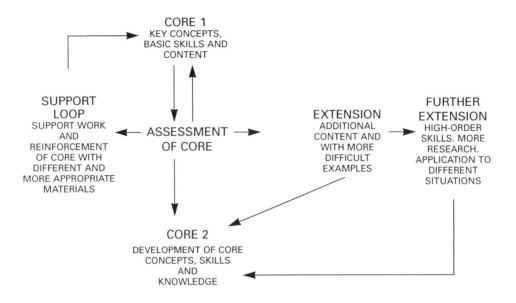

**Figure 5.1** A model for core extension

## DIFFERENTIATION

Differentiation has become a buzz word, a convenient portfolio term for an issue that has always been with us. HMI and OFSTED reports have frequently drawn attention to the scandal of undifferentiated lessons. The concept is relatively simple, but is not like learning a new trick in order to get it right. It is a word, like 'creativity' and 'enrichment', that trips off the tongue and means different things to different people. Creating the conditions to achieve it is a difficult task and differentiation, for all its common currency, is an ellusive goal. The word keeps surfacing because the detailed practice to produce it is so hard to sustain and the solutions to the problem are very challenging. Even when the goal seems within reach, something may happen that turns the apparent success into an illusion.

Schools and colleges should offer children a basic entitlement to a broad range of curriculum experiences. However, the differences in pupils' natural abilities and interests mean that their individual needs will differ as they progress through this curriculum. To provide for their basic entitlement, pupils in the same group must have learning opportunities matched to their particular needs and abilities. The process of assessing individual needs and responding with appropriate learning experiences is called differentiation.

A curriculum that is differentiated for every pupil will: build on past achievements; present challenges to allow for more achievements; provide opportunity for success; and remove barriers to participation. This means teachers devising tasks appropriate to the range of abilities, aptitudes and interests of their children, regularly reviewing pupils' progress through observation, discussion and testing, which leads to variation in the tasks pupils have to undertake, and then offering support for individual work, both in person and through the ready availability of appropriate resources. Differentiation has become a live issue because schools experience difficulty in coping effectively with the wide range of pupils that come through their doors. The spread of comprehensive schools and the increasing access to mainstream schools of pupils who have quite acute learning or behavioural difficulties have highlighted an issue that has always been there. Mixed-ability groups, taken for granted and, on the whole, well executed in primary schools, are seen by some as a threat to standards in the secondary school. There has been a long-running debate about standards, which shows no sign of diminishing. For some, the solution lies in the return to grammar schools, which for those who thrived in them were often a great success, but there was also a great deal of underachievement in the old tripartite system, just as there undoubtedly is in many a comprehensive school today. To link differentiation to pupils at the extremes of the normal distribution curve of ability is to miss the point. No mass of 60 per cent of pupils in the middle range are doing well in school. Some are, but many are not. Differentiation is not primarily about helping slow learners or disaffected pupils. Differentiation is not just about stretching the clever child. Differentiation is about all children, because all children are different, and one of the fascinating aspects of being a teacher is this very fact of human variation and all its attributes. Differentiation then is the process by which curriculum objectives, teaching methods, assessment methods, resources and learning activities are planned to cater for the needs of individual pupils. Differentiation is making the whole curriculum accessible to the learning needs of the individual. This is as good a definition as any.

With this definition in mind, differentiation then becomes the linchpin of the entitlement curriculum. It is meaningless if access is not available. The other important point about this definition is the emphasis on the individual. This could prove to be a much more helpful emphasis in categories such as 'slow learner', 'average', 'bright' or 'gifted', although it would be foolish to suggest that these categories are meaningless. All children are marked by individuality; they think differently, they behave differently, they learn differently, they come from different backgrounds and they bring different skills, attitudes and abilities with them. This is both the joy, but also the great challenge for the busy teacher. For this reason, I regard differentiation as an issue affecting all pupils of every age in every kind of school in every kind of grouping. Figure 5.2 summarises some of these differences.

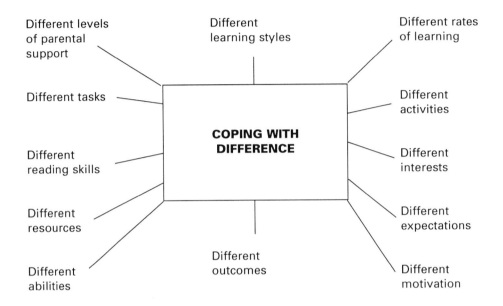

**Figure 5.2** Coping with difference

Teachers use two major ways of differentiating learning activities. The first is commonly called *differentiation by task*. After establishing curriculum objectives for a class activity, the next step is to develop tasks that help individual pupils achieve these objectives. Many factors affect the difficulty of the task, and these include:

- the required accuracy for measurements,
- how familiar the pupils are with the materials and apparatus to be used,
- how familiar the pupils are with the concepts and vocabulary involved in the investigation,
- the extent to which a teacher leads or prompts pupils,
- the number and types of variables involved in any investigation.

Secondly, there is *differentiation by outcome*. This involves setting a common task for the class. The task is designed so that every pupil understands what is required. They use their knowledge and understanding to achieve success at different levels. The more able should be expected to:

- plan and carry out more complex work,
- use more difficult concepts in planning their work,

- make more accurate measurements,
- complete more stages in an investigation,
- record results more precisely,
- express findings in more sophisticated vocabulary.

The emphasis should be on effective teaching styles which assist a creative learning environment, in which differentiation is most likely to happen (see Tables 5.1 and 5.2).

**Table 5.1** Effective teaching styles which assist differentiation

Humour
Praise
Positive attitude and high expectations
Responsive to pupil ideas
Clear organisation
Clear instructions and objectives set
Resources available
Teacher allows time for pupils to reflect
Teacher intervenes to check progress
Teacher intervenes to diagnose difficulties
Teacher intervenes to move work forward
Teacher resists over-demanding pupil
Teacher finds opportunities to create a 'community of learning' in the classroom – some whole class work and group work and other teaching strategies.
Teacher varies length of tasks to provide:
  (a) some long, open-ended opportunities enabling all to work at their own pace;
  (b) complete opportunities so that reflection/completion/feedback are all within a short period.
Teacher involves pupils by explaining objectives, work plan, expected outcomes, success and assessment criteria – giving pupils the opportunity to plan the pathway through their own work – and anticipates the difficulties of different pupils.
Teacher does detailed planning (preferably in collaboration with others).
Teacher gives short crisp demonstrations/punchy introductions.
Teacher sets varied and realistic time-scales for the work.
Teacher has planned support, consolidation and extension activities.
Teacher keeps up-to-date records, to identify what children have achieved and where to move next.

**Table 5.2** The learning environment in which differentiation is most likely to happen

It arises from a fully planned work scheme to which a team of people have contributed.
Differentiation as an issue is highlighted by the format of the work scheme, e.g. column on a grid; the special needs of slow learners and able pupils are planned for in advance.
Teaching/learning approaches are an integral part of the planned scheme.
A wide variety of teaching/learning styles is deployed (see Table 5.1).
Students are involved in the planning of their work.
Active steps are taken to organise the room and to manage the situation to minimise low-level demands on teacher by pupils. Pupils are given ready access to their current work, both in storage and wall displays.

Teacher actively seeks opportunities to know pupils and their work.

Assessment is linked to the aims/objectives of the work scheme. Students are aware of success criteria. Teacher's recording methods reflect wide range of assessment opportunities .

Control is fully established so that the efforts of all are directed to the planned task.

There is a comfortable atmosphere – humour, praise, positive enthusiastic attitude on part of teacher – defined by one colleague as 'cheerfulness'.

Independent learning is encouraged.

There is a mixture of open-ended and limited-time tasks, the latter requiring a specific outcome.

A wide range of stimulating and easily and independently accessible resources (print, pictures, videos, artefacts) lead to creative, reflective, speculative responses appropriate to the range of ability encompassed within the class.

On the point of vocabulary, Table 5.3 shows a typical short scheme of work based on tree studies, which are commonly used for children's investigations in the environment, whether it is in a city park or a rural village school. However, many children are capable of much more advanced language, which should be encouraged in every subject, in this case science. The question, therefore, is which of the words from the two tables would one use?

**Table 5.3** The use of vocabulary

## Tree studies – Specific objectives

(a) Compare differences in stem and bark structure.

(b) Discover how trees are related to other organisms e.g. birds and insects.

(c) Identify and make a collection of the leaves of trees.

(d) Devise a method of measuring the heights of trees.

(e) Compare shapes and sizes of trees.

(f) Relate trees to uses of their wood.

(g) Make a histogram of the types of trees found.

(h) Use a simple key to identify tree leaves, buds and winter silhouettes.

(i) Compare plants growing under trees with those growing in open areas.

Useful words for expressing objectives

| Simple | More complex |
|---|---|
| Identify | Compare |
| Make | Discriminate |
| Describe | Generalise |

| | |
|---|---|
| *Find* | *Devise a method* |
| *Collect* | *Justify* |
| *Measure* | *Discover* |
| *Examine* | *Formulate hypotheses* |
| *Prepare* | *Propose reasons for* |
| *Classify* | *Deduce* |
| *Draw* | *Relate* |
| *Construct* | *Prove* |
| *Estimate* | *Infer* |
| *Plot a graph* | *Predict* |

In order to implement enrichment, extension and a differentiated curriculum in the classroom, we must remember that students learn in many different ways. The wide range of needs of children found in an ordinary classroom is more likely to be met if a wide range of teaching styles is adopted. Not all styles suit all subjects, but many teachers have a narrow repertoire. Teachers are as prone as anyone in any other profession to getting into a rut. Even the best ideas can be overdone and, having advocated the individualisation of learning, we must remember that that can be overdone, and it may be that an inspired explanation heard by all and shared by the whole class would be of most benefit.

In an interesting article entitled 'What Is Teaching?', Paul Hirst (1971) drew an important distinction between the concept of teaching as an enterprise which included organisational ploys and all the incidentals and necessary preliminaries that teachers may find themselves involved in during the course of a day's work, including sharpening pencils and opening windows – and the concept of teaching as a specific activity which is directly connected to the enhancement of learning. Almost any activity could take on a teaching function. For example, if a teacher was trying to demonstrate certain basic skills such as how to sharpen pencils, then the performance could be seen as part of a specific teaching activity, but such demonstrations would be marked off from preliminaries of related activities by such remarks as, 'This is the way to do it', or 'If you hold the pencil this way, you will find it easier'. The fresh criterion for genuine teaching is that a teacher must be acting with a clear intention of bringing about learning.

There are, however, two other conditions that must hold if an activity is to be classed as teaching. Firstly, the pupils must be learning. The teacher may be undertaking an activity with the intention that the pupils should learn, but if in fact they are not learning, either because they are switched off or because they have already mastered the skill or item of knowledge, no teaching is strictly involved. Research shows that this is often the case with gifted and talented children. Secondly, the teacher cannot really be teaching unless what he or she is doing will aid the learning process. To assist busy teachers in providing the right effective teaching style to aid differentiation, it is useful to give gifted and talented children the learning style inventory below, which will then enable teachers to match how these children learn to what they are able to provide.

## Learning style inventory

This survey is designed to explore the way you prefer to learn. Look at the four statements across each row and decide how they refer to you. Give four marks for the statement nearest to you, three to the second, two for the third and one for the statement least appropriate to you. There are no right or wrong answers.

| | a | b | c | d |
|---|---|---|---|---|
| 1. | I like to get involved | I like to take my time before acting | I am particular about what I like | I like things to be useful |
| 2. | I like to try things out | I like to analyse things and break them into parts | I am open to new experiences | I like to look at all sides of issues |
| 3. | I like to watch | I like to follow my feelings | I like to be doing things | I like to think about things |
| 4. | I accept people and situations the way they are | I like to be aware of what is around me | I like to evaluate | I like to take risks |
| 5. | I have gut feelings and hunches | I have a lot of questions | I am logical | I am hard working and get things done |
| 6. | I like concrete things, things I can see, feel or touch or smell | I like to be active | I like to observe | I like ideas and theories |
| 7. | I prefer learning in the here and now | I like to consider and reflect about them | I tend to think about the future | I like to see the results of my work |
| 8. | I have to try things out for myself | I rely on my own ideas | I rely on my own observations | I rely on my feelings |
| 9. | I am quiet and reserved | I am energetic and enthusiastic | I tend to reason things out | I am responsible about things |

Educational reform, which is prevalent throughout the world, is not about allowing able learners to stagnate in an age-grade lock step classroom. If schools were willing to adopt flexible models of grouping that allowed students' needs to dictate practice, rather than administrative convenience or fashions of the times, the needs of all children might be better met. If schools were willing to alter instruction based on need as readily as they are willing to move children around administratively, the needs of all children would be better met. Improving the quality of education for all requires that teachers be sensitive to the needs of all, and plan educational experiences accordingly. Quality of opportunity and quality of treatment in education, however, are not the same, nor should they be. In any profession, the needs of the client dictate the nature of the prescription. Although high-quality service should be available to all, the nature and organisation of these services should vary, on the basis of diagnosed need. Education can ill afford to level its services lest the bitter pill of mediocrity be absorbed in the bloodstream of all our students.

Educating the most able children in appropriate ways is a challenge that society must take seriously. We cannot afford to foster underachievement, disaffection and alienation amongst these children. Even now, national and international comparisons on achievement, drop-out rates and delinquency data suggest that a disproportionately high percentage of the most capable children are not maximising their considerable potential.

# CHAPTER 6

# The Parent/Child/Teacher Model

> After you understand about the sun and the stars and the rotation of the earth, you may still miss the radiance of the sunset. (A. N. Whitehead)

When Michelangelo went to Rome to see the Pope prior to being employed to build the Great Dome of St Peters and paint the Sistine Chapel, he took a reference with him which said: 'The bearer of these presents is Michelangelo the sculptor, his nature is such that he requires to be drawn out by kindness and encouragement but if love be shown him and he be treated really well, he will accomplish things that will make the whole world wonder.'

This chapter is primarily for parents who are seen as partners with the professionals in the educational process to make children whole. However, the chapter will be helpful to all concerned in the education of children; and, of course, many teachers are parents themselves. It is based on the assumption that children are the most precious natural resource in the world and that parents are a child's most important teacher, particularly in the early crucial years. Parents need to be familiar with the language of education and to know what is going on in schools. If very young children could articulate their feelings, they might well say, 'Learning about myself and the world around me is my work. Your part is loving and supporting me'. Good parenting, then, is an essential part of educating children, but the parent of a child with gifts and talents also faces obstacles, risks, challenges, errors and joys. This is where it is essential for teachers and parents to be sensitive to each other's problems and to help one another.

This chapter will emphasise some practical approaches to the education of gifted and talented children and aims to be different from the previous chapters (see Painter, 1980; Freeman, 1985, 1991; White in Freeman, 1985; and Clarke, 1988).

I shall begin the discussion by looking at what every child needs. The healthy status of an individual is considered to be governed by the biological integrity and the dynamics of the social cultural factors within the individual's environment. Children's health, owing to their dependence, is greatly influenced by the health of the family unit and the quality of the relationship between members of the family and the wider world. The fact that education has recognised the influence of such factors upon a child's learning is reflected in official educational documents, which consistently emphasise the relationships between the child's home, community and school. Space does not allow further discussion of the health of a child, but remember that the World Health Organisation defines health as 'the state of complete physical, mental and social well-being, not merely the absence of disease and infirmity'. Health is a vital aspect in the total development of all our children, and parents have an important role to play in ensuring that children have adequate sleep, nutrition, exercise and peace of mind.

The interaction between emotions and an individual's needs is outlined admirably in Maslow's hierarchy of human needs (1954); see Figure 6.1.

**Figure 6.1:** Maslow's hierachy of human needs

Maslow's model asserts that it is necessary to satisfy basic needs before higher-level needs can be met, and suggests that emotions reflect the level of satisfaction experienced by an individual. These levels are dynamic, and are dependent upon the individual's capacity to meet the various levels of needs. It is essential to meet a child's physiological needs first, and, unfortunately, too many children are bogged down at the base of the pyramid. Secondly, children need to feel that the world is organised and predictable so that they can feel safe and secure. Thirdly, children need to feel loved and to have the opportunity to love others. Fourthly, children need to have self-esteem, as well as the esteem of other people. When these needs are met, motivation will direct behaviour towards self-actualisation, which means living up to one's fullest and unique potential. Before gifted and talented children can acquire the skills of competence they will need to learn the skills to develop their effective base. Both parents and teachers need to integrate their skills to meet the fundamental needs of their children.

In the same way, Rimm's hierarchy of cognitive needs (1989) states that the 3Rs (to which I would add environment) sit at the base of the hierarchy of intellectual needs. These basic skills are the prerequisites for the middle levels of the hierarchy (knowledge and its applications) and, in turn, analysis, synthesis and evaluation of ideas are required for the top level of the hierarchy, (creative production). All gifted and talented children should be encouraged to move towards the higher levels of the hierarchy. However, if they have not mastered the basic skills, they are likely to perform like children with average, or below-average, abilities and therefore will not be identified as gifted. Teachers have a vital role in looking at the whole child.

## THE EARLY CRUCIAL YEARS

The concept of gifted infants is unwarranted. The reality is that there is only the potential for giftedness, and this requires an optimum environment for full development.

One of the ways to help very young children with potential is to admit them to school earlier than is normal and, indeed, most children in England now have the opportunity to go to school soon after the age of four. Research studies (Reynolds et al., 1976; Proctor et al., 1986), although varying in their criteria for selecting students and in their methods for ascertaining success, have consistently been in favour of early admission to school. It is, however, important for these children to be well screened before being admitted. Some teachers are very cautious because early entry into school may cause personal as well as academic and social problems. Parents and teachers need to work closely together and carefully consider some of the variables before making the decision.

- *Reading readiness.* This skill is crucial to early school success and, of course, many gifted children are able to read prior to school entrance.

- *Gender.* Boys mature later and it is often young girls who are more physically mature and, therefore, are ready to go to school earlier than boys.
- *Eye/hand coordination.* Children admitted earlier should have reasonable motor skills, otherwise the inability to draw, cut materials and write could put unnecessary stress on a young child
- *Health.* The child who has a history of good health is more likely to attend school regularly and be able to concentrate.
- *Social, emotional and physical maturity.* It is essential that the child is really ready to appreciate and gain from going to school early. This is largely the decision of the parent, in consultation with the teacher, because it involves the support of the family (see the section on acceleration in Chapter 4).

Many parents are sensitive observers of their own children and know when their children have special talents. These parents can inform teachers that their youngster has unique abilities, and a joint evaluation can then take place (see the parent questionnaire on pp.56–7). Teachers may be able to help parents by discussing the following:

(1) Is your child curious about the world and keen on exploring and discovering its meaning?
(2) Is your child interested in the whys, the wheres, and the hows as well as always asking questions?
(3) Is your child really well above his or her age level in ability and possibly even self-taught?
(4) Does your child have a good vocabulary?
(5) Did your child start to walk and talk earlier than average?
(6) Does your child show special abilities in such areas as problem solving, art, music and even mathematics?
(7) Does your child appear to be unusually attentive and able to concentrate?
(8) Does your child show advanced motor skills and is your child good at physical activities?

An honest discussion of these characteristics would help in identifying children with the potential for giftedness and in coming to a decision about early admission to school.

To find out whether a child has gifts and talents is one thing, but we have to remember that this is a continuing process. A child's needs, interests and behaviour change with time, and their growth and development are uneven. Therefore, continuous assessment and recording of behaviour, in discussion with the school, are very important. Likewise, children should be given every opportunity to be exposed to a variety of experiences. For example, a child needs the experience of playing the piano to show outstanding talent in that field. The more opportunities a child has to take part in a wide range of activities, the more likely it will be that his or her gifts and talents will be detected. This means being flexible in the use of time to accommodate interests and encourage perseverance.

We now know that the environment begins to exert an influence on a child before birth and that a favourable pre-birth environment will enhance intellectual growth and development. Young children are genetically unique and their intelligence has a strong inherited base, but that intelligence is manifold and more than the narrow quality measured by IQ tests. We also know that children need an optimum environment in order to maximise their potential, and that domains other than the cognitive must be considered in our search for the early precursors of giftedness. Education in the early years in general has long practised individual learning by children, creating a unique environment for each child. Ideally, this should carry through to the secondary phase of education, although this is harder because there is some incompatibility between an individual's needs and the demands of society for a flow of trained manpower. However, individual learning is sound both educationally and biologically.

Flexibility of mind, and an exceptional immaturity at birth compared with other animals give humans a unique capacity for development. Interaction with a stimulating environment, including language, is critical to the mind's development. Burton White's Harvard project studied the development of several hundred children over some twelve years (White et al., 1979). It was found that the average Western environment contains all that is needed for the development of most human abilities during the first few months of life. There is also evidence that the rate of achievement of abilities in these first months can be substantially increased. For example, children can learn to use their hands as reaching tools by three and a half months, rather than by five.

The Harvard project discovered that by the end of the second year of life, infants have gained two-thirds to three-quarters of all the language he she or they will ever use in ordinary conversation for the rest of their life, including all the major grammatical elements in their native language and a receptive vocabulary of about 1000 words. In addition, infants at this age will have developed thinking skills, attitudes towards learning and a full range of social skills. Brierley (1978) states that, at the age of five, the brain has reached 95 per cent of its adult weight and suggests that half of the intellectual growth of a child is complete. Parents, who are a child's most important teachers, should be aware of this rapid development of intelligence during the early years, as well as the crucial development stages, and also that a child craves experience.

The brain's timetable of development may be altered by experience. For instance, at about the age of three a child is able to start searching systematically for experiences. Children at play is therefore a serious business. It is about work learning, not about relaxation, and toys need to look and sound as real as possible (for example, a graded abacus and a toy telephone). This is why pre-school education has lasting benefits into adulthood.

The effects of early nutrition on the brain's mature capabilities are also crucial. Poor nutrition in pregnancy may not be so important as nutrition in the first two or three years of life, because the foetus may be protected from poor nutrition, but, by the end of the first two years of life, the growth spurt of the brain is over. Relatively lethargic children may be so for reasons of poor diet; they are likely to be less open to stimulation and not develop well. The brain contains a model of the world built up through the senses. This model depends on the quality of a child's experience. Each of us has different models. Information from the senses is scanned against the model and decisions are taken as a result of the scanning process. A child needs to explore, talk and play with others to refine the model. A poor environment creates a poor state of mind that learns to expect little out of life. Evidence suggests that memory is stored rather diffusely within the brain tissue and cognitive development is a reflection of interest and maturation, as well as of biological and inherited ability.

In this age of computers and space travel, our understanding of the mind is only just beginning, and much more research is needed. Scientific evidence now indicates that only the left half of the brain is capable of fully expressing its thoughts in words; and the right side of the brain has its own separate train of thoughts, which are not in words. Though these non-verbal thoughts are a crucial part of our personality and abilities, they continue to be ignored and misunderstood because they are so difficult to translate into words. Because the right side of the brain is capable of controlling actions, remembering things, solving problems and developing our emotional selves, it fully qualifies as a mind by itself. In spite of this fact, we continue to look at the mind as a single entity that thinks only in words. When you look at a human brain, it is obviously a double organ consisting of two identical-looking hemispheres joined together by bundles of nerve fibres called the *corpus callosum*. Yet the human mind resides strictly in one of the hemispheres. What could the equal amount of brainpower in the other hemisphere be doing? Most of the organs of the body are in pairs and evolutionary forces simply do not allow the kind of waste that would be represented by having one hemisphere sit idle. In fact, measurements of the rate of metabolism of the two hemispheres indicate that both are doing the same amount of work.

Contemporary understanding of human brain functions establishes that each side of the brain is unique and that brains in general are specialised. Experts argue about the degree of specialisation (Herrmann, 1987), but there is general agreement on the fact of specialisation. For example, there is agreement on the concept of dominance. Although the body is symmetrical in terms of organ duality (we have two eyes, two ears, two hands, two feet and two brain hemispheres), in the use of these dual organs, there exists a general asymmetry. In other words, we use one to a greater degree than the other. When combined, the concepts of specialisation and asymmetry (or dominance) produce within each human being a distribution of specialised preferences that affect general behaviour. Specifically included is an individual's learning style. This has important implications for both parents and teachers of children, in that intelligence is no longer one-dimensional but rather includes the notion of multiple intelligences Each individual is a unique learner with learning preferences and avoidances different from those of other learners.

All this points to the need to provide optimum conditions for all children from birth and we should not be satisfied until all children are born into homes where parents have the knowledge, skills and financial resources to meet all the needs of the growing child. The years 0–5 are perhaps the most crucial; then the brain is undergoing maximum growth and is probably at its most plastic. For example, the brain is built to mop up language incredibly quickly. Babies are born with the left (language) hemisphere larger than the right. Therefore language, like food, is a basic need, and it is essential that children are talked to and not treated to 'shut-up' answers. A child's experiences in the early primary years seem to matter for the rest of life, because of the physical changes in the cortex, which are perhaps unchangeable. However, deprivation cannot be solved by schools alone. The influence of the streets, television, homes and youth organisations is crucial. Parent/school liaison is of the greatest importance and is a difficult art. The school should not undermine the dignity and authority of the parents with the children.

## WHICH SCHOOLS WILL PROVIDE THE BEST EDUCATION FOR MY CHILD?

The following list of what makes an effective school can assist parents when making choices:

- *Qualities of pupils*
  A mixture of backgrounds or abilities seems to be best, although the key appears to be to have a large enough concentration of pupils who come to school with good academic skills. Too great a concentration of children with poor skills makes it more difficult for the rest of the items in this list to occur.
- *Goals of the school*
  There is strong emphasis on high standards in both academic and non-academic areas and on high expectations. These goals are clearly stated by the administration and shared by all the staff.
- *Organisation of classrooms*
  Daily activities are to be structured, with a high percentage of time spent in actual group teaching (as opposed to planning and organising for instruction or in behaviour management). There is a variety of curriculum options for gifts and talents to be identified and encouraged.

- *Praise*
  Pupils are praised for good performance, for meeting expectations and for really trying. The school is structured but warm (see Maslow's hierarchy of needs in Figure 6.1, p.113).

- *Homework*
  Homework is assigned regularly and marked quickly. Effective schools assign considerably more homework than do less effective schools.

- *Discipline*
  Most discipline is handled within the classroom, with relatively little resort to sending children to the head teacher. In really effective schools, however, not much class time is actually spent in discipline because the teachers have very good control of the class. They intervene early in a potentially difficult situation rather than imposing heavy discipline afterwards.

- *Teacher experience*
  Teacher education is not necessarily related to the effectiveness of schools, but teacher experience is, presumably because it takes time to learn effective class management and teaching strategies. This learning process also requires specific guidance and training from experienced teachers. The importance of mentors for probationary teachers cannot be stressed too much. The staff believe that the education of children is the joint responsibility of staff and parents and they encourage community involvement wherever possible.

- *Resources*
  The school has sufficient facilities, resources and staff to be flexible in its organisation and the staff are aware of and sensitive to the needs of all children.

- *Surroundings*
  The age or general appearance of the school building are not critical, but maintenance in good order, cleanliness and attractiveness do matter. The school ethos starts with the receptionist and the appearance of the entrance.

- *School leadership*
  Clear values are shared and readily stated by senior school staff. The academic emphasis of the school is apparent in all school activities, in the allocation of funds and in priorities of time usage.

- *Responsibilities for children*
  Children are more likely to be given real responsibilities in individual classrooms and in school as a whole. The children are actively involved in their own learning and are given the opportunity to demonstrate their talents.

- *The whole child*
  The school develops the whole child – body, mind and spirit – and shows a concern for the cultural and social backgrounds of children.

## HELPING CHILDREN AT HOME

- Meet children's needs for love and controls, attention and discipline, parental involvement and training in self-dependence and responsibility.
- Help gifted children to face feelings of difference arising from their exceptional abilities. These feelings might otherwise create emotional problems, disruptive behaviours or withdrawal from the frustrating situation.
- Present consonant parental value systems.
- Become involved in early task demands, such as training children to count, tell the time, to use correct vocabulary and pronunciation, to locate themselves and get around their neighbourhood, to do errands and to be responsible.
- Emphasise early verbal expression, reading, discussing ideas, poetry and music.
- Read to children.
- Emphasise doing well in school.
- Encourage children to play with words. Even in such common settings as a car ride or shopping trip, word games such as rhyming, opposites and puns can be used to their full advantage.
- Provide a variety of books, magazines, puzzles and games to promote use of the imagination, logical thinking, drawing inferences and making predictions.
- Help gifted and talented individuals to become critical viewers and readers by discussing the mass media and literature.
- Avoid disruption of family life through divorce or separation, and maintain a happy, healthy home.
- Because able children often have an awareness of adult problems such as sex, death, sickness, finances and war, which their lack of experience makes them unable to solve, offer reassurance in these areas.
- Encourage children to play an active role in family decisions. Listen to their suggestions, applying them wherever possible. For example, when planning a trip or vacation, have them participate in decisions about places, routes, food and activities, and assign important tasks appropriate to their abilities – such as map reader on a trip or bookkeeper of the family budget.
- Explore ways of finding and solving problems by asking questions, posing hypotheses, discussing alternative solutions and evaluating those alternatives. Personal and family situations may be used, as well as the larger social issues of the town, the country or the world.
- Help children relate to friends who may not be so gifted. Although gifted children should recognise their abilities, they should also learn to put them into perspective. They need to look for strengths in friends as well as for

ways to share their abilities productively.

- Provide good books, magazines and other aids to home learning, such as encyclopaedias, charts and collections.
- Take children to museums, art galleries, educational institutions and other historical places where background learning may be enhanced.
- Be especially careful not to 'shut up' the child who asks questions. In particular, do not scold for asking, or imply that this is an improper or forbidden subject. You may, however, insist that questions not be asked at inappropriate times, or require the child to rephrase a question so as to clarify it. Sometimes questions should not be answered completely, but the reply posed as a question that sends the child into some larger direction. If you cannot answer the question, direct the child to a resource that can.
- Avoid 'pushing' a child into reading, 'exhibiting' him or her before others or courting undue publicity. On the other hand, seek in every way to stimulate and widen the child's mind, through suitable experiences in books, recreation, travel and the arts.
- Prize and praise efforts and accomplishments. Support children when they succeed as well as when they don't. Create an atmosphere where risk taking is all right.
- Encourage children to challenge themselves. Because of their superior abilities, the gifted and talented often work at only partial capacity and still succeed. This approach to learning, however, may ultimately create difficulties because the individuals may acquire extremely poor learning habits which they may not be able to overcome when they are sufficiently challenged.

## STIMULATING ACTIVITIES TO DO WITH YOUR CHILDREN AT HOME

- Play Scrabble using only words around a theme (for example, 'farm', 'Christmas', 'weather'). Children must give the rationale for words used.
- Pick a household item and invent ten new uses for it apart from the obvious.
- Design the perfect broom, vacuum cleaner or sink.
- Introduce children to global education by listening to a foreign radio station, picking up a foreign newspaper and exploring it with the child, listening to foreign music, creating a dish from a foreign country using products similar to the native recipes.
- Plan a trip and mention problems that arise. Let the children solve the problem with yellow pages, newspapers and maps.
- Write letters to manufacturers praising or complaining about their products. Make suggestions for improvements. Include a catchy commercial jingle. Discuss commercials for obvious and hidden messages. Enter a manufacturer's contest.

- Invite an elderly member of the family to discuss old times and life fifty years ago. Design a family crest or flag depicting family history and symbols of the family's value system. Prepare a motto to accompany the crest. Work out a family tree. Keep a diary of family or personal events and make each entry different, such as a poem, a slogan, an illustration, song lyrics.
- Investigate various forms of communication in your home – body language, facial expressions, conversation, animal communication, media. Design your own code of communication.
- Chart the routine of animals and plan a change in habits. Record the changes in behaviour in the development of a habit. Design the perfect fictitious household pet, borrowing characteristics of other animals.
- Get the child to redesign his or her bedroom to accommodate hobbies and interests. Allow suggestions for architectural and structural changes on paper. Ask the child to find a new way to make a bed, decorate a window or set a table, and give the rationale for the changes.
- Listen to different kinds of music – jazz, calypso, swing, as well as classical. Discuss mood and interpretation of music and encourage free dance expression to the music. Rent or borrow an instrument and investigate musical patterns.
- Discuss a favourite TV programme and plan two plots and sub-plots for the characters. Relate the characteristics of the characters to those of friends and relatives. Discuss the plausibility of the present plots and relate them to their own personal experiences.
- Star gaze and investigate astronomy. Learn about the calendars of different cultures (Hebrew, Chinese). Create a new month with a new holiday.
- Watch a new sport. Invent a sport with logical rules, uniforms and equipment.
- Scour the newspapers for local problems and plan logical solutions. Write letters to the Editor.
- Learn a new craft.
- Ask children to condense a film, book or TV programme into four sentences or four words.
- Create and illustrate a cartoon strip featuring original animated characters.
- Devise a weather station for recording conditions and predictions. Plan novel ways of conserving energy and water based on your findings.
- Devise a new maths value system and plan equations in your system. Explore unfamiliar operations on a calculator.
- Learn about perennial and annual plants and plan a timetable for flowering.
- Plan a simple chemical experiment from household items. Explore the chemical components of household items and foodstuffs. Discuss chemical changes in food and additives.
- Solve crossword puzzles or anagrams and construct your own. Plan riddles and pantomimes.

- Explore infrequently visited spots in your home for 'antiques' and discuss the value of items. Consider economic concepts such as appreciation/depreciation. Have the children plan a car boot sale and evaluate the items for sale.
- Read current world news items. Analyse the articles for solutions and discuss how the possible solutions will filter down to affect their lives.

## LOOKING AT THE WHOLE CHILD

This book has to some extent followed the traditional model of defining who we are talking about, identifying the children and providing a special programme. It also suggests a new model, which should have as its basis the provision of a rich, stimulating experience to extend all children to the highest potential of which they are capable in a climate that fosters creativity and allows some freedom of choice. Because gifted behaviour is observed to emerge under these conditions, sensitive teachers, with parental support, will provide opportunities for further development.

From whatever point of view one contemplates the educational scene, one sees at once a marked division between the mind and the spirit. Certain things are not quantifiable and, with the emphasis on cost effectiveness and efficiency, it is necessary to guard against the decline in the quality of life as a whole. The mind has to do with the ability to deduce cause and effect, to follow a logical argument, to reason, to calculate, to memorise facts, to infer and deduce. It is these attributes more than any others that have enabled the creation of Concorde, but also of the nuclear bomb. The spirit is different. It has to do with fears and joys, enthusiasms and apathies, loves and hates. It is this side of our nature, more than our minds, that decides when we shall release the bomb and whom we should kill with it. It accounts for the horrors in Northern Ireland as well as the compassion of Oxfam. It accounts for the driving force of men such as Gandhi and the whole army of creative people. The differences between mind and spirit reveal themselves in the average classroom in simpler ways. There is, for example, the difference between the mechanical process of reading and the enjoyment of what is read; between the mechanics of musical notation and sensitive playing and singing; between writing on a prescribed topic from notes on a blackboard and telling someone in your own personal written words about something that has excited you; between lessons on perspective and giving a child the urge to draw or paint; between the teacher who tries to find out why a child is ill-behaved and remove the cause and the teacher who obtains a purely superficial result by sarcasm; between the teacher who ranks and grades children solely on their achievements and the one who makes allowances for handicaps and judges effort; between the head of a school who sees the timetable and the framing of school rules as the main task and the one who, by the use of recognition, expectation and encouragement, draws the best out of both colleagues and pupils.

Of course, one cannot divide the curriculum into things of the mind and things of the spirit. Indeed, I talked earlier about the holistic approach to a child's education. If a child is good at arithmetic but loathes it, the failure in my terms is one of the spirit. However, the current education system tends to attach more importance to things of the mind that can be measured, to subjects that traffic in these things, to the teachers who can teach them and to the children who are good at them, than to activities that deal mainly with the spirit and whose manifestations defy measurement.

The neglected affective area of education, which in addition to developing spirituality includes self-concepts, self-esteem, values and moral thinking, social adjustments, altruism and motivation, is essential for the development of well-rounded, fulfilled and outgoing students. Most gifted and talented children are well able to understand moral issues and to discuss them. Parents have a vital role to play here because teachers are under considerable pressure with large classes, testing and the National Curriculum to implement. To build self-esteem, schools should look at children's positive attributes and tell children of their capabilities and worthwhileness. Developing children's self-concept should be a goal of every school because a good self-concept motivates children to higher aspirations and achievements. There are many perceptions of self, including:

- *Body self* – which includes understanding changes and the use and misuse of the body.
- *Sexual self* – understanding sexual development and the role of sexuality in relationships.
- *Vocational self* – making contributions to society, lifestyles and developing awareness.
- *Social self* – understanding others' perspectives and their role in relationships, coping with conflicts, working with others and making sense of others.
- *Moral self* – the making of judgements, resolving moral dilemmas, taking action on issues.
- *Self as a learner* – understanding strengths and weaknesses and reflecting on approaches to learning.
- *Organisation self* – becoming an active member of the school, giving and gaining benefits.

Given time, commitment and opportunities, schools can teach a humanistic, caring curriculum that includes exposing children to the problems of the elderly and handicapped and involving them in community service, raising money for worthwhile projects, recycling materials in school (which raises awareness of environmental issues) and debating pollution, overpopulation, AIDS, abortion and other issues of real concern.

I am hoping to create individualised learning kits that will enrich the curriculum in some of the areas discussed. Table 6.1 sets out the basis of a holistic curriculum over and above that provided by the National Curriculum. The five areas would make for a genuinely enriching curriculum.

**Table 6.1**   The basis for a holistic curriculum

| Body | Mind | Spirit | Relationship | Environment |
|---|---|---|---|---|
| Exercise | Thoughts | Beliefs | Family | Soil |
| Food | Feelings | Values | Friends | Plants |
| Illness | Ideas | Experience | Community | Animals |
| Health | | Faith | Society | Weather |
| | | | | Water |
| | | | | Air |

# CHAPTER 7

# Resources and Policies

> Do not, then, train youth to learn by force and harshness, but lead them to it by what amuses their minds so that they may discover the peculiar bent of the genius of each.
> (Plato)

> Never mistake knowledge for wisdom. One helps you make a living: the other helps you make a life.
> (Sandra Carey)

Until recently, education in Britain has been dominated by two key concepts – growth and equality. This situation is now changing and the emphasis must switch to a sustained concern for the quality of the enterprise.

With the demise of the Schools Council Gifted Children Project, the National Association for Able Children in Education (NACE) was established to help teachers turn potential into performance by enriching and extending the curriculum for more able children. This work now continues in conjunction with the National Association for Gifted Children.

NACE challenges the contemporary viewpoint that quality can be obtained by standardising the curriculum, concentrating on the so-called 'basic skills' and developing new systems, monitoring and assessment – moves that inevitably lead to greater centralised control of schools and the curriculum. Quality requires the full recognition of individual differences and the wide range of society's needs. Quality in education must relate to the quality of life itself and cannot be achieved without opportunities for specialism and individual enrichment. The achievement of quality ultimately depends on the skills of the teaching profession and the cooperation received from both parents and the community as a whole.

There is a tendency to equate the needs of industry with those of education and to use industry as a model for the educational system. It is possible that certain procedures from industry could improve quality in education. Two in particular stand out: firstly, by better design, products can be made more useful, efficient or long-lasting; secondly, production techniques can be modified in order to create better-quality output in relation to cost. As far as education is concerned, quality could be improved, firstly by modifying the objectives and goals of the end product and, secondly, by working on the techniques, processes and structures of the enterprise so that the desired objectives can be more clearly achieved. It is, however, also important to recognise that, although we can draw industrial parallels of this kind, there are well. Firstly, pupils are not raw material to be moulded into any shape that educational designers consider appropriate. Each child is a unique individual with wishes and wills that must be taken into full consideration in any decisions about what should be taught and to which pupils, or how much learning should be structured and presented. Secondly, pupils, unlike raw materials in factories, do not spend all their time in one place. What they do at home and elsewhere, their leisure activities, the TV programmes they watch, the various people they meet and talk with, have just as profound an influence on the quality of their education as formal schooling, which takes up only 17 per cent of their waking life. Hence a concern for educational quality cannot simply be left as an objective for teachers and administrators. It must be the concern of the whole community.

If class teachers are to give the most effective help to all children in their care, then they need all the support that it is possible to provide. Many pupils are learning efficiently and are developing their individual talents. However, there is concern that some of the more able children are underachieving and one of the objectives of NACE and other organisations has been to produce resources to assist teachers concerned about helping the more able children to reach their potential.

## RESOURCES

### Useful addresses

**Aquila Magazine for Able Children** – published by Thomas Nelson and Sons, Hammersmith, London.
**Bildung und Begaben e.V., Wissenschaftszentrum** – PO Box 20 1448, D5300 Bonn 2, Germany.
**Centre for Creativity, Innovation and Leadership** – materials mainly about innovative thinking and leadership. Available from the Associate Director, Hilda Rosselli, Human Sciences Building 414, University of Florida, Tampa, FL 33620, USA.
**Cheshire LEA** – *Management Guidelines – Identifying and Providing for Our Most Able Pupils* (1996), County Hall, Chester.
**Children of High Intelligence** – 6 Upper Harley Street, London NW1 4PS.
**DES Library Bibliography No. 39: Gifted Children (HMSO)** – lists books and articles. A free copy can be obtained from the Department for Education and Employment, London.
**Direct Education Supplies** – includes teacher's manual and 31 activity packs. Available from E. de Bono, 35 Albert St., Blandford, Dorset.
**European Council for High Ability** – produces an excellent journal, and newsletters, holds conferences and undertakes research.
**Exceptionality Education, Canada** – a new journal edited by Judy Luport of the University of Calgary to encourage scholarly exchange of ideas.

**GIFT** – courses for children. 5 Ditton Court Road, Westcliff on Sea, Essex.

**Gifted Education International** – a useful journal edited by Belle Wallace and published by AB Academic Publishers, Bicester, Oxon, UK.

**Hampshire LEA** – has produced valuable 'Material for the Able Child' (MACH) and also, as part of its Curriculum Differentiation Initiative, the publication 'Matching the Curriculum to the Needs of the Individual' (Hampshire County Council, The Castle, Winchester, Hants).

**The Mathematical Association** – 295 London Road, Leicester LE2 3BE.

**National Association for Able Children in Education** (NACE) – 'Able and talented children's lives can be enriched and their thinking skills extended through stimulating learning activities which can be enjoyed by all children.' NACE seeks to achieve this by:

- Encouraging the provision of an enabling climate for learning within the classroom in order to create opportunities for special abilities to manifest themselves and be recognised.
- Supporting those who have a professional concern for the education of able and talented children through a termly newsletter.
- Disseminating good practice through an annual conference and other activities.
- Promoting the education, training and professional development of teachers.
- Seeking to secure appropriate resources for enrichment and extension activities in schools.
- Encouraging the study of able and talented children.
- Liaising with the DFEE, LEAs and any other organisation engaged in further similar aims to this association.

NACE is based at Westminster College, Oxford OX2 9AT.

**National Council for Educational Technology (NCET)** – encourages supported self-study and has a consultancy and an information service. Sir W. Lyons Road, Science Park, University of Warwick, Coventry CV4 7EZ.

**National Association for Gifted Children (NAGC)** – an association of parents, teachers and other adults interested in the development and education of gifted children. It was founded in 1966 and helps parents and children through its ever-growing number of branches all over the UK. Membership categories include family, individual, student and corporate. It offers newsletters, help with bright children and counselling. National Centre for Children of High Ability and Talent, Elder House, Milton Keynes, MK9 1LT.

**NAGC USA** – 4175 Lovell Road, Suite 140, Circle Pines, NY 55014, USA.

**NFER & Nelson** – tests. Darvil House, Oxford Road, Windsor, Berks.

**Nottinghamshire County Council** – *Able Child* – *Compendium of Ideas* (1994).

**Odyssey of the Mind** – Mastery Education Corporation, 85 Main Street, Waterwon, MA 02172, USA.

**Philosophy for Children** – Institute for the Advancement of Philosophy for Children, Montclair State College, Upper Montclair, NJ 07043, USA. Also developed by Brunel University.

**The Potential Trust and Questors** – the aim of the Trust:

> To help children with special needs, whose needs arise from a high degree of unfulfilled potential in one or more areas – intellectual, practical, aesthetic, creative, social, personal – by complementing the provision already made for such children by parents and schools, in co-operation with other individuals and organisations working in the same field.

The Trust runs interesting holidays for able children. Shepherds Close, Kingston Stert, Chinnor, Oxon OX9 4NL.

**Primary Thinking Skills Project & Top Ten Thinking Tactics** – Questions Publishing Co., 27 Frederick Street, Hockley, Birmingham.

**Pullen Publications Limited** – produces enrichment and extension material. 121 London Road, Knebworth, Herts SG3 6EX.

**Queensland Association for Gifted and Talented Children** – PO Box 121 Ashgrove, QLD4060, Australia. Queensland is the only state in Australia which has a full team of some eight or nine inspectors concentrating upon curriculum extension and enrichment for the talented and able.

**Roeper Review** – PO Box 329, Bloomfireld Hills, MI 48013, USA.

**Shell Education Service** – Shell UK Limited (Shell Mex House, Strand, London WC2R ODX) has produced a number of study projects related to industry, science and technology and these are available from Bankside House, West Mills, Newbury, Berks RG14 5HP.

**Somerset Thinking Skills course** – Staplegrove Road, Taunton, Somerset, TA1 1DG.

**Talented** – a recommended newsletter that includes ideas and resources. Available from UNE Armidale, CB Newling Centre, Armidale, NSW, Australia.

**Trillium Press** – a major American publisher that specialises in enrichment and extension publications and materials. PO Box 209, Monroe, NY 10950, USA.

**Wirral Able Child Centre** – Caldy Grange Grammar School, West Kirby, Wirral.

**World Council for Gifted and Talented Children** – membership details, biennial proceedings from world conferences and resources available from 210 Lindquist Centre, University of Iowa, IA 52242-1529, USA. Has developed an international diploma for teachers of gifted and talented children. The world conferences provide a world forum for research, materials and the exchange of ideas.

Few of the materials purporting to be differentiated and to offer genuine enrichment over and above the content of the National Curriculum have been rigorously evaluated and this is a challenge for future research.

**Books**

Helpful books for teachers will be found in the Bibliography. See especially: Bloom (1985), Clarke (1988), Davis and Rimm (1989), Denton and Postlethwaite (1985), Eyre and Marjoram (1990), Feldhusen (1985), Freeman (1985), Gallagher (1985), Leyden (1985), Maltby (1984), Ogilvie (1978), Renzulli (1977), Sternberg and Davidson (1986), Teare (1996a,b), and Wallace (1983).

### Aids to teaching more able children

The following can be used in any order that meets your needs:

- concept mapping
- task analysis
- darts
- developing writers
- computers
- talk
- mastery learning
- readability
- your own educational material
- behaviour management
- pupil motivation
- baselining
- metacognition
- support for learning
- supported self-study
- beginnings, endings, questioning
- assessment
- marking written work
- classoom organisation
- senior management team
- Open University foundation course books
- mentors, learned societies, colleges

## POLICIES

In order to offer an effective service, governors, parents, teachers and other involved professionals need to be clear about school policies in general, but in particular about policies for gifted and talented children. Policies should form part of the overall curriculum plan for the school. Gifted and talented children should be enabled to work at the highest level, both for the good of others and for their own satisfaction. It is generally recognised that those of exceptional high ability, in whatever area of human endeavour, require rich, challenging experiences to achieve fulfilment.

## Devising a policy

A policy to meet the needs of these pupils should include ways of identifying them and monitoring their progress, as well as making provision that is consonant with the National Curriculum but also enriches and extends it. It should make clear what strategies the school will follow in the case of a child displaying general giftedness across the curriculum or specific talents. This will mean addressing such issues as acceleration, enrichment and extension of the curriculum. Such developments should take place on a whole-school basis, taking into account those children who are considerably more able than their peers, as well as the generally accepted 10 per cent who would be identified nationally as more able.

The policy should address the following:

(1) Consistent terminology and definition. For Britain, a definition might well be as follows:

Gifted and talented students are those whose functioning is at least at the upper end of or above that normally associated with that key stage; and whose abilities are so well developed or so far in advance of their peer group, that a school has to provide additional learning experiences to develop, enhance and extend the identified abilities.

This definition should be accompanied by a profile of the child that will assist the teacher to consider the first stage of identification. The school then needs to consider – Have we any children like this? How are we meeting their needs? (see the questionnaire on p.132)

(2) Methods for screening, registering and monitoring the progress of pupils with these abilities.

(3) Advice on identifying gifted and talented children.

(4) Aims and objectives, which should reflect the idea that the provision for able children should be seen as an aspect of provision for all pupils. Therefore, it is important to raise the awareness of all staff, and for the management to provide training and guidance to enable all teachers to meet the needs of these children.

(5) Staff agreement on the appropriate procedures for recognition, provision and assessment of children. It is important that each member of staff has a sense of ownership.

(6) The provision of opportunities for pupils to practise and develop their particular abilities, and to get together to share and develop their talents.

(7) A directory of useful local expertise that might assist these children in their work, including the appointment of mentors.

(8) Enabling these pupils to work, for the most part, with their peers in ways that lead to social and emotional maturity and help them to build strong relationships with others.

# Questionnaire on departmental provision for more able pupils

Please answer the following questions by ticking the appropriate box or boxes.

1. Do you have any 'more able' pupils in your department/class?

| YES | NO | DON'T KNOW |
|---|---|---|
|  |  |  |

2. Which procedures do you use, if any, to identify able pupils?

| TESTS | PROGRESS REPORTS | TEACHER ASSESSMENT | PARENT REPORTS | NONE |
|---|---|---|---|---|
|  |  |  |  |  |

3. What provision, if any, do you make for able pupils?

| WITHDRAWAL GROUPS | ENRICHMENT MATERIAL | ACCELERATION | OTHER | NONE |
|---|---|---|---|---|
|  |  |  |  |  |

4. Are there any specific difficulties in providing for able pupils in your department/class?

| LARGE CLASSES | STAFF SHORTAGE | LACK OF RESOURCES | OTHER | NONE |
|---|---|---|---|---|
|  |  |  |  |  |

5. Do you make additional arrangements to accommodate the more able pupils?

| CLUBS | PARENTAL INVOLVEMENT | AFTER-SCHOOL ACTIVITIES | EDUCATIONAL VISITS | NONE |
|---|---|---|---|---|
|  |  |  |  |  |

6. Do you have special resources for the more able child?

| YES | NO | DON'T KNOW |
|---|---|---|
|  |  |  |

7. Is there anyone responsible for able children in your department?

| YES | NO |
|---|---|
|  |  |

(9)  The development of a collection of appropriate resources.

(10) Records about the children identified and their progress.

### The role of the school coordinator

Once a policy has been agreed, it is essential to appoint a school coordinator. This person needs highly developed perception and communication skills. In many schools, this role falls on the Special Education Needs Coordinator, who has more than enough to do. Such a coordinator would have the following role in the school:

- to initiate the formulation and revision of the school policy;
- to consult with the senior management of the school and all the staff;
- to call for nominations from staff, parents and students (see the referral form below);
- to maintain awareness of parental attitudes in Britain and abroad and of external agencies, to disseminate information to all staff, and to advise on the availability of in-service courses in this area of expertise;
- to identify, invite and match mentors to students and to arrange an initial meeting between students, mentors and parents;
- to organise the expertise of staff and devise a talent pool of advisers and inspectors of the LEA;
- to liaise with the parents of gifted and talented children;
- to initiate and maintain the agreed system of profiling, including testing;
- to establish systems for cross-phase liaison;
- regularly to follow up students' progress with mentors, supervising teachers and students.

## REFERRAL FORM FOR GIFTED, TALENTED OR UNDERACHIEVING CHILDREN

I wish to draw your attention to ...........................................................................................

in ................................................................................................(Class or Tutor Group)

Please find attached the following:

1. Check list
2. My written description of the child's classroom performance
3. Letter from parent
4. Test results
5. Photocopied evidence from the child's written work
6. Other

Signed ...................................................................................................................................

## National Curriculum Issues

Attainment targets are now age-related in law, creating problems in managing provision for very able pupils. Such pupils may make rapid progress to a point beyond their key stage. If schools make provision for such pupils while at the same time keeping them with their age group peers, technically they would be breaking the law. Therefore, there should be a procedure in the school policy to avoid this, such as advancing the child into the next key stage. This assumes that the pupil will continue to function at an advanced level and will not 'plateau out' in skill or knowledge acquisition and that the pupil can cope socially and emotionally with such acceleration (see the section on acceleration in Chapter 4). Another option would be to apply to have the National Curriculum disapplied (although this may or may not be allowed), which would certainly involve the school in an extra burden of administration. The pupil will carry only the equivalent age-related financial weighting, not that of the accelerated key stage. Because these two options pose difficulties, a third option is the provision of extension work. It means considering the following questions:

- How can this be planned, managed and delivered?
- How can we extend the way children are involved in their own learning?
- How can children be given even more responsibility for their own learning?
- How can we extend our cross-phase links to encompass tutoring?
- How can the library service help to supplement our resources?
- Have we a targeted plan for resource buying?

Meeting the needs of able children by using planned educational programmes, tutors from other establishments, targeted resources and the library as a multi-media resource base would solve many National Curriculum issues.

## Policy in action

One of the great pleasures of undertaking in-service courses around the country is that schools then implement policy and a plan of action to support teachers and gifted and talented children in schools. This has also meant that a number of schools have sent me materials of policy in action. I am grateful for permission to use the following three policy papers from schools around Britain. The schools vary from rural to urban, from primary to secondary, as well as in approach and level of success to date. They are examples for others to emulate.

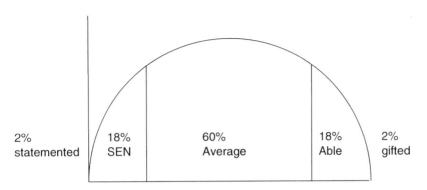

2% statemented  |  18% SEN  |  60% Average  |  18% Able  |  2% gifted

*Snodland Primary School*
*School policy on the able child*

*Definition*

Any definition by its very nature will be subject to criticism and individual interpretation. 'Gifted' is a term which can be used to refer to children at the extreme range of ability (the top 2 per cent) within one subject or across several.

As a staff, we feel that the definition of gifted should include the able top 20 per cent in the standard distribution curve of ability: a proportionate number to the children whose needs are met in our special needs policy.

This means that on average, in a class of 30, there should be about six children who fall into this category. Within our 14 classes we are looking at identifying and providing for 80 to 90 children.

Of all the definitions we have examined, that which best covers our requirements is David George's (1992):

Gifted and talented children are those who in some aspect of human potential and/or achievement are far more advanced beyond that which would normally be expected.

This broad, general definition covers potential achievement in intellectual ability, creativity, leadership, visual and performing arts and psycho-motor ability, and thereby provides many opportunities for children to have access to our provision of extension and enrichment.

*Identification*

There are a number of possible methods of identification. All of them have weaknesses and limitations. It is sensible, therefore, to use as wide a net as possible, incorporating many strands of thought, and not to rely too heavily upon the results of any one method.                                    (Teare, 1996a)

*Methods of identification*

Norm Referenced Tests

These can be useful as an initial screen to supplement and counterbalance teacher observations. They may not identify those with motivational or observational problems.

Checklists – General Characteristics

Useful as a guide on what to look for. They may not be relevant in individual cases.

Creativity Tests

These may offer the chance to show quality of imagination and divergent thinking in those overlooked by conventional tests. These are difficult to assess and time-consuming to administer.

*Teacher Observation and Recommendations*

These are essential: the trained eye of the teacher should know the child, but may miss some who do not conform to accepted standards of work or behaviour; who present motivational or behavioural problems; with belligerent or apathetic attitudes; who come from homes which do not share the school ethos.

## Creative Learning Environment

The all-important ingredient, encouraging all children to explore their talents, exercise their developing capacity to learn and understand, and to reach the highest potential of which they are capable.

## Provision

Provision for the able child will focus on three areas: material, organizational and pedagogic.

## Material

Children will have access to further reading material, extra source material of all kinds to facilitate deeper and more detailed study of the theme in hand. Individual learning packs or assignment sheets from a variety of sources will be readily available to enrich the normal supply of classroom materials as well as the class teacher's own produced materials.

## Organizational

Provision to enrich or extend the curriculum may include extra individual or group help *in situ* by a visiting teacher; withdrawal from the normal class to take part individually or as a group in curricular studies; promotion for part or whole of the week regularly/occasionally to work with a more advanced class; visits to exhibitions, museums, field centres; visits by poets, painters, etc.

## Pedagogic

Pedagogic provision lies at the heart of enrichment and extension. It represents the personal element upon which all depends. The inspirational mentor, the gifted teacher, can offer more than any amount of inanimate material and organization. Staff INSET, both present and future, will help to ensure that this aspect of provision remains firmly fixed as part of this policy and our overall school philosophy.

## Recommendations

In order to recommend a child for able provision, teachers will need to provide a record of their observations. Observation and recording of such children need to be as objective as possible, and it will therefore help to have a structured framework within which such observations can be formulated.

a. Evidence from school tests
– any child who scores 115 or more on any of the NFER tests
– any child who scores 120 or more on the intelligence test
– any child whose reading age is one year or more above their chronological age.
b. Teacher referral checklist
– any child who has a majority of ticks in the exceptional category.
c. Any other evidence not covered in a. or b., but which is considered by the class teacher to be indicative of above-average ability.
This evidence to be submitted on referral form to the Able Child Coordinator.
Examples of identification material:

Norm Referenced Tests                                   NFER English
                                                        NFER Maths
                                                        NFER Reading
                            Hunter Grundin Reading Intelligence Test.
Checklist of General Characteristics        From 'Teaching Bright Pupils',
                            Nottingham University School of Education
Creativity Test             TCT – DP/TSD Z Testsheet from Urban and Jellen.
Referral Form and
Teacher's Checklist.


## Cedars School (urban comprehensive)

*Extending our teaching and our students' learning*

Introduction
Learning is the main function and central activity of the school and each teacher constantly seeks to maximise learning for each student. GCSE, TVEI and the National Curriculum have all brought with them a reconsideration of the ways we teach and the ways in which our students learn. Moreover, recent involvement with Geoff Grounds, David George and the IAS has made us focus more sharply as a whole school on developing our teaching and learning styles.

Rationale
We believe that our prime task is to create the most appropriate learning environment so that students are able to go as far and as fast as they can. To achieve this, we need to create the widest possible variety of learning opportunities with differentiated activities that recognise different learning rates, styles, interests and abilities.

Policy
Each curricular team and each member of staff is responsible for actively developing varied learning opportunities for our students, for ensuring that students have access to as wide a range of resources as possible, and for seeking ways of increasing the student centred nature of work. However, developments need to be centrally co-ordinated so that we learn from each other, avoid unnecessary duplication of effort and maximise resources, especially the precious resource of staff time.

Intended outcomes

• Staff will provide a greater variety and improved balance of flexible learning opportunities.
• Tasks will be better geared to meeting the needs of individual students and provide greater opportunity for developing higher order skills.
• Students will take greater responsibility for their own learning.
• Student enjoyment of learning and motivation will increase, and we shall be even more successful in translating potential into performance.
• Students, especially the more able, will be given more demanding activities.
• Students will be presented with a wider range of resources.
• There will be a greater opportunity for individual work with students.
• Larger group sizes will be reduced wherever feasible. There will be an increase in small group work.

- There will be increased emphasis on study skills and on learning how to learn.
- Resource areas, in particular the library, will undergo major change to facilitate student learning.
- Certain departments will provide specialised opportunities for independent learning.
- There will be greater dialogue within and between departments about teaching and learning.
- There will be greater shadowing of students and observation of colleagues' lessons.
- Increased use will be made of ancillary staff to support teachers.
- We shall work more closely with our middle schools.
- There will be a smoother transition between Year 11 and Year 12 work.

Monitoring

Monitoring will be partly by departmental review and partly through review by the Curriculum Group. It will focus on discussion as to developments, using the department sheets in section 5 as a basis for both review and forward planning. A yearly summary of progress will be produced.

Further points
(1) It is recognised that much staff development will occur through developing teaching and learning styles.
(2) The school is now a member of the National Association for Curriculum Enrichment and copies of its publications (*School Policy on Able Children, Identification, Writing Curriculum Enrichment Materials, Resource Lists for Mathematics, Science and Technology*) are available in the library.

## Faringdon School

Faringdon School, a comprehensive in a market town, developed its interest through the enthusiasm of its deputy head. The resulting approach was different, but demonstrates well the flexibility of enrichment and extension as a method of provision.

(1) It started by accident. Some INSET days are tedious, others change your life. Listening to David George at Nene College, Northampton, opened up a whole new way of thought to me and made me realise how inadequate it was simply to provide a 'top set' as a school response to the more able child.
(2) I joined the school to the National Association for Curriculum Enrichment, of which David George is the President, read their leaflets and attended their annual conference. Dr George came very willingly to Faringdon to speak to the staff to raise awareness and challenge them.
(3) One or two little things started to happen. I ran a lunchtime Spanish group in two half hours a week for about ten months, in an attempt to catch the last of the O levels. It was a mixed group of able third years and interested lower sixthformers. I did not exclude anyone from opting in from my top set. Consequently some did (whom I would not have advised), some did not (who could have coped). In the event, the grades were A, B, 2 x C, 2 x D and 3 x U. Inconclusive – but a start and some highly motivated children, one of whom has gone on to gain an A in GCSE Latin.

(4) While our pupils are required to find their own work experience at the end of their fourth year, the head of science has been able to make the most of some superb placements locally in scientific and electronic establishments. This has led to the pupils doing extended work experience in these places and being given specific projects to do by the companies. In some cases, the pupil has designed or created something which has been adopted by the company. In one case, having not followed the course at school, a boy entered for A level computer studies at the last minute (in the fifth form) and got a grade C, as well as nine GCSE passes.

(5) An electronics club started at lunchtime. A parent provides regular and significant input to this. The attendance has revealed certain youngsters whom one could describe as 'talented' rather than 'more able'. We have been surprised at the skill shown by some of our pupils in this area which has not come out in other sections of the curriculum.

(6) A pupil has come to light in our first year who is years ahead in French – he is functioning at good fourth-year standard. We have, therefore, taken the plunge and decided to teach him individually using a variety of materials: books, videos, cassettes and computer programmes. A pupil of this type raises all sorts of curriculum questions about the phrase in everybody's brochure which says 'we value the education of each child equally'.

(7) In response to my circular colleagues have approached me offering to run Latin as an interest/exam course and there is talk of reintroducing a competitive chess club.

(8) A colleague is working with a pupil deemed to be 'on strike' by his primary school who, according to tests, appears to have a very high IQ. At the moment, on an individual basis, computer programmes – both doing and writing – are being put in his way with good results.

(9) Now that I have passed on the overall responsibility for special needs in the school to a fellow deputy head, I am able to devote more time to finding a school attitude to this phenomenon. I have now circulated the staff with some ideas for purchasing some self-support and self-marking materials, for contacting parents and for making more use of lunchtimes and extension materials. We have in existence a cross-curriculum group, the Special Needs Curriculum Group, where this can be debated.

Thus we have arrived at take-off point!

Richard Arrowsmith

See also the published school policy of King's School, Ottery St Mary, Devon, in George (1995).

## PROGRAMME EVALUATION

An evaluation of programmes for the gifted and talented should be based on the areas and objectives of the programme and be diagnostic. Various points of view should be sought and involve the children, parents, teachers and management of the school. The evaluation scheme should be on-going and thereby allow quick reaction to faults and strengths. This will enable planning, development and accountability from a natural sequence of educational objectives. It must be recognised that the evaluation of these programmes requires awareness of the problems associated with assessing higher-level objectives, the unsuitability of conventional standardised tests and the practical demands on time, money and trained personnel. The evaluation could take the form of pre and post tests, and teacher, parent and children questionnaires. Above all, ask the children; they have so much to contribute (Endean and George, 1982).

## WORKSHOP TASKS FROM INSET COURSES

(1)  Identify a group leader and secretary.
(2)  Prepare an OHP and report back to all course members.
(3)  Discuss strategies for identifying the more able children in your school.
(4)  What are the principal issues to be addressed in establishing provision for the special needs of more able students in the secondary comprehensive/primary school?
(5)  How can these issues be tackled successfully?
(6)  What are the most effective ways of supporting colleagues in providing enrichment and challenge in the classroom?
(7)  Plan a strategy of identification of underachievement and examine causes of failure to achieve in these individuals.
(8)  How is it possible to stimulate bored, underachieving teenagers? How can subjects such as science, history, geography and English be made to come alive and challenge bright underachievers?
(9)  Discuss a future school policy for the children in your school and suggest five areas for implementation.
(10) How do you identify a child who is an early second language learner?
(11) In the light of your school's experience of gifted and able children, share thoughts on the challenges they present to you, your school and (where you have the knowledge) their parents. Your recent observation of a gifted/able child in your own school may be relevant to the discussion.

# EPILOGUE

Sometimes I look about me with a feeling of complete dismay.
In the confusion that afflicts the world today, I see a
Disrespect for the very values of life.
Beauty is all about us, but how many are blind to it!
They look at the wonder of this earth – and seem to see nothing.
Each second we live in a new and unique moment of the universe,
A moment that never was before and will never be again.
And what do we teach our children in school?
We teach them that two and two make four, and that Paris is
the capital of France.
When will we also teach them what they are?

We should say to each of them: do you know what you are?
You are a marvel. You are unique.
In all of the world there is no other child exactly like you.
In the millions of years that have passed, there has never
been another child like you.
And look at your body – what a wonder it is!
Your legs, your arms, your cunning fingers, the way you move!
You may become a Shakespeare, a Michelangelo, a Beethoven.
You have the capacity for anything.
Yes, you are a marvel. And when you grow up,
Can you then harm another who is, like you, a marvel?
You must cherish one another.
You must work – we must all work – to make this world worthy
Of its children.

(Pablo Casals)

# Bibliography

Barbe, W. B. and Renzulli, J. S. (eds) (1975) *Psychology and Education of the Gifted.* John Wiley, New York.

Betts, G. (1985) *Autonomous Learner Model: For the Gifted and Talented.* Autonomous Learning Publications and Specialists, Grealey, Co.

Binet, A. and Simon, T. (1905) 'Méthodes nouvelles pour le diagnostic du niveau intellectuel des anormaux'. *L'Année Psychologique* 11, 191–244.

Birch, J., Tisdall, W., Barney, D. and Marks, C. (1965) *A Field Demonstration of the Effectiveness and Feasibility of the Early Admission to School.* University of Pittsburg.

Blakeslee, T. R. (1980) *The Right Brain.* Macmillan, London

Bloom, B. (1974) *Taxonomy of Educational Objectives.* McKay, New York.

Bloom, B. S. (1985) Developing Talent in Young People. Ballantine Books, New York.

Bono, E. de (1973) *CORT Thinking.* Pergamon, New York.

Bono, E. de (1985) *Six Thinking Hats.* Little Brown, Boston.

Bragget, E. J. (1992) *Pathways for Accelerated Learners.* Hawker Brownlow, Sydney.

Branch, M. and Cash, A. (1966) *Gifted Children: Recognising and Developing Exceptional Ability.* Souvenir Press, London.

Brierley, J. K. (1973) *The Thinking Machine.* Heinemann, London.

Brierley, J. K. (1978) *Growing and Learning.* Ward Lock, London.

Brody, L. and Benbow, C. P. (1987) 'Acceleration Strategies: How Effective Are They?' *Gifted Children Quarterly* 31, 105–110.

Burt, C. (1975) *The Gifted Child.* Hodder & Stoughton, London.

Butler-Por, N. (1987) *Gifted Underachievers.* John Wiley, Chichester.

Clark, B. (1988) *Growing Up Gifted.* Merrill, Columbus, OH.

Clarke, G. (1988) *Identification of Gifted Pupils.* Longman, London.

Cockcroft, W. (1982) *Mathematics Counts.* HMSO, London.

Coleman, L. (1985) *Schooling the Gifted.* Addison-Wesley, Reading, MA.

Colengelo, W. L. and Davis, G. A. (1991) *Handbook of Gifted Education.* Allyn & Bacon, Needham Heights, MA.

Cox, J. et al. (1985) *Educating Able Learners.* University of Texas Press, Austin, Texas.

Czikszenmihalyi, M. and Robinson, R. E. (1986) 'Culture, Time and the Development of Talent'. In R. J. Sternberg and J. E. Davidson, *Conceptions of Giftedness.* Cambridge University Press, Cambridge.

Czikszenmihalyi, M., Rathunde, K. and Wholen, S. (1993) *Talented Teenagers – The Roots of Success and Failure.* Cambridge University Press, Cambridge.

Davis, G. A. and Rimm, S. B. (1989) *Education of the Gifted and Talented*. Prentice Hall, New Jersey.

Denton, C. and Postlethwaite, K. (1985) *Able Children: Identifying Them in the Classroom*. NFER-Nelson, Windsor.

DES (1977) 'Gifted Children in Middle and Comprehensive Schools'. HMI Series, *Matters for Discussion* 4. HMSO, London.

DES (1978) 'The Development of Sporting Talent in Children of School Age'. Circular 16/78 (Joint Circular). HMSO, London.

DES (1985a) *Better Schools*. HMSO, London.

DES (1985b) *The Curriculum 5–16*. An HMI Series. HMSO, London.

DES (1986) *Gifted Children*. DES Library Bibliography No. 39. HMSO, London.

Dunn, R., Dunn, K. and Treffinger, D. (1992) *Bringing out the Giftedness in the Young Child*. John Wiley, Chichester.

Edwards, B. (1992) *Drawing on the Right Side of the Brain*. Harper Collins, London.

Endean, L. and George, D.R. (1982) 'Observing Thirty Able Young Scientists'. *School Science Review*. 73 (135).

Eyre, D. and Marjoram, T. (1990) *Enriching and Extending the National Curriculum*. Kogan Page, London.

Feldhusen, J. F. (ed.) (1985) *Towards Excellence in Gifted Education*. Love Publishing, Purdue.

Feldhusen, J. F. and Kolloff, P. B. (1981) 'A Three-Stage Model for Gifted Children'. In D. Classen et al., *Programming for the Gifted and Talented and Creative*. University of Wisconsin.

Feldhusen, J. F. and Treffinger, D. J. (1985) *Creative Thinking and Problem Solving in Gifted Education*. Kendall/Hunt, Dubuque.

Feldman, D. H. (1982) *Developmental Approaches to Giftedness*. Jossey-Bass, Chicago.

Flack, G. (1990) *Creativity*. G. T. News, University of Colorado.

Freeman, J. (ed.) (1985) *The Psychology of Gifted Children*. John Wiley, Chichester.

Freeman, J. (1991) *Gifted Children Growing Up*. Cassell, London.

Gagne, F. (1985) 'Giftedness and Talent: Re-examining a Re-examination of the Definitions'. *Gifted Children Quarterly* 29, 103–112.

Gallagher, J. J. (1985) *Teaching the Gifted Child*. Allyn & Bacon, New York.

Gardner, H. (1983) *Frames of Mind*. Basic Books, New York.

Gardner, J. W. (1961) *How Can We Be Excellent and Equal Too?* Harper & Row, New York.

Gear, G. (1978) 'Effects of Training on Teachers' Accuracy in the Identification of Gifted Children'. *Gifted Children Quarterly* 21, p. 90.

George, D. R. (1990) 'The Challenge of the Able Child'. Cambridge Journal of Education 20(2).

George, D. R. (1992) *The Challenge of the Able Child*. David Fulton, London.

George, D. R. (1994) *Enrichment Activities for More Able Children.* Chalkface, Milton Keynes.

George, D. R. (1995) *Gifted Education.* David Fulton, London.

George, W. C. (ed.)(1979) *Educating the Gifted: Acceleration and Enrichment.* Johns Hopkins University Press, Baltimore, MD.

Getzels, J. and Jackson, P. (1962) *Creativity and Intelligence.* John Wiley, New York.

Gold, M. (1979) 'Acceleration: Simplistic Gimmickry'. In W. C. George (ed.) *Educating the Gifted.* Johns Hopkins University Press, Baltimore, MD.

Gross, M. U. M. (1993) *Exceptionally Able Children.* Routledge, London.

Guilford, J. P. (1967) *The Nature of Human Intelligence.* McGraw-Hill, New York.

Guilford, J. P. (1977) *War Beyond the IQ.* Creative Education Foundation, Buffalo, NY.

Harvey, S. and Steeley, J. (1984) 'An Investigation into Relationships among Intelligence, Creative Abilities, Extra-Curricular Activities, Achievement and Giftedness in a Delinquent Population'. *Gifted Children Quarterly* 28, 73-9.

Heller, K. A. and Feldhusen, J. F. (eds) (1988) *Identifying and Nurturing the Gifted: An International Perspective.* Hans Huber, Toronto.

Heller, K. A., Monks, F. J. and Passow, H. A. (eds) (1993) *Research of Giftedness and Talent.* Pergamon Press, Oxford.

Herrmann, N. (1987) *The Application of Brain Dominance Technology to the Training Profession.* 7th World Conference, Salt Lake City.

Hitchfield, E. M. (1973) *In Search of Promise.* Longman, London.

HMSO (1977) *Gifted Children in Middle and Comprehensive Secondary Schools.* London.

HMSO (1985a) *Good Teachers.* London.

HMSO (1985b) *Ten Good Schools.* London.

HMSO (1988) *Secondary Schools – An Approach.* London.

Howe, J. A. (1990) *Sense and Nonsense about Hothouse Children.* British Psychological Society, Leicester.

Howley, A., Howley, C. and Pendarvis, E. (1986) *Teaching Gifted Children: Principles and Strategies.* Little, Brown & Co., Boston.

Jellen, H. G. and Urban, K. K. (1989) 'Assessing Creative Potential World-wide'. *Gifted Education International*, 6, 78–86.

Jones, C. A. (1986) *Developing Physical Skills to Full Potential.* National Association for Curriculum Enrichment Publications, Newcastle upon Tyne.

Kamin, L. G. (1974) *The Science and Politics of IQ.* Penguin, Harmondsworth.

Kerry, T. (1983) *Finding and Helping the Able Child.* Croom Helm, London.

Kirschenbaum, R. (1987) 'Enrichment Programming for Gifted and Talented High School Students'. *Roeper Review* 10, 117–18.

Kitano, M. and Kirby, D. (1986) *Gifted Education: A Comprehensive View.* Little,

Brown & Co., Boston.

Klein, R. (1982) 'An Inquiry into Factors Related to Creativity'. *Elementary School Journal*, 82, 256–266.

Leyden, S. (1985) *Helping Children of Exceptional Ability*. Croom Helm, Beckenham.

Lock, R. and Jay, G. (1987) 'Self-Concept in Gifted Children: Differential Input in Boys and Girls'. *Gifted Children Quarterly* 31, 9–14.

McAlpine, D. S. (1988) *Creativity: Teaching Processes and Teaching Implications*. NACE Publications, Northampton.

Magoon, R. A. (1981) 'A Proposed Model for Leadership Development'. *Roeper Review* 3, 7–9.

Maker, C. J. (1982a) *Curriculum Development for the Gifted*. Aspen Systems Corporation, Aspen.

Maker, C. J. (1982b) *Teaching Models in Education of the Gifted*. Aspen Systems Corporation, Aspen.

Maltby, F. (1984) *Gifted Children and Teachers in Primary Schools*. Falmer Press, Brighton.

Marland, S. (1972) *Education of the Gifted and Talented*. Report to Congress. US Office of Information, Washington DC.

Maslow, A. H. (1954) *Motivation and Personality*. Harper & Row, New York.

Mason, P. ( 1987) *The Social, Educational and Emotional Needs of Gifted Children*. Cicely Northcote Trust, London.

Meeker, M. N. and Meeker, R. (1986) 'The SOI System for Gifted Education'. In J. S. Renzulli (ed.) *Systems and Models for Developing Programmes for the Gifted and Talented*. Creative Learning Press, Mansfield Centre, El Segundo, CA.

NAGC (1989) *Help With Bright Children*. Northampton.

NAGC (1990a) *Survey of Provision For Able and Talented Children*, Northampton.

NAGC (1990b) *According to their Needs*. Northampton.

National Society for the Study of Education (1979) *The Gifted and the Talented: Their Education and Development*. NSSE, London.

NCC (1989) *A Curriculum For All – Curriculum Guidance 2*. London.

NCC (1990a) *The Whole Curriculum – Curriculum Guidance 3*. London.

NCC (1990b) *Core Skills*. London.

Newland, T. E. (1976) *The Gifted in Socioeducational Perspective*. Prentice Hall, New Jersey.

Novak, D. and Goodwin, B. (1984) *Learning How to Learn*. Cambridge University Press, Cambridge.

Ogilvie, E. (1973) *Gifted Children in Primary Schools*. Macmillan, London.

Painter, F. (1980) *Meeting the Needs of the Gifted in Schools*. Pullen Publications, Hertford.

Painter, F. (1984) *Living with a Gifted Child*. Souvenir, London.

Parry, S. J. (1977) 'The Concept of Excellence in Sport'. In NATFE Conference

Report.

Pegnato, C. and Birch, J. (1959) 'Locating Gifted Children in Junior High Schools'. *Exceptional Children* 25, 300–304.

Plowman, P. D. (1981) 'Training Extraordinary Leaders'. *Roeper Review* 3(3), 13–16.

Postlethwaite, K. (1988) *Organising the School's Response*. Macmillan Education, London.

Povey, R. (ed) (1980) *Educating the Gifted Child*. Harper & Row, London.

Proctor, T. B., Black, K. N. and Feldhusen, J. F. (1986) 'Early Admission of Selected Children to Elementary School: A Review of the Research Literature'. *Journal of Education Research* 80(2).

Renzulli, J. S. (1977) *The Enrichment Triad Model: A Guide for Developing Defensible Programs for the Gifted and Talented*. Creative Learning Press, New York.

Renzulli, J. S. (1988) *The Multiple Menu Model for Developing Differentiated Curriculum for the Gifted and Talented*. Univ. of Connecticut, New York.

Renzulli, J. S., Reis, S. M. and Smith, L. H. (1981) *The Revolving Door Identification Model*. Creative Learning Press, New York.

Renzulli, J. S., Smith, L., White, A., Callahan, C. and Hartman, R. (1977) *Scale for Rating the Behavioural Characteristics of Superior Students*. Creative Learning Press, New York.

Reynolds, M. C., Birch, J. W. and Tuseth, A. A. (1976) 'Research on Early Admission'. In W. Dennis and M. Dennis (eds) *The Intellectually Gifted*. Grune & Stratton, New York.

Rimm, S. B. (1989) *Underachievement Syndrome: Causes and Cures*. Apple Publishing. Co., Waterdown, WI.

Rimm, S. B. (1990) *How to Parent a Child So Children Will Learn*. Apple Publishing Co., Waterdown, W1..

Rimm, S. B. (1990) 'Underachievement Syndrome: Causes, Preventions and Cures'. *Exceptionality Education, Canada*, 1(1).

Rogers, C. R. (1962) 'Towards a Theory of Creativity'. In S. J. Parnes and H. F. Harding (eds), *A Source Book for Creative Thinking*. Scribners, New York.

Shore, B.M. (1981) *Face to Face with Giftedness*. 1st Yearbook of 1981 World Conference, World Council for Gifted Children, Calgary.

Shore, B. M. (1991) 'Building a Professional Knowledge Base'. *Exceptionality Education, Canada*, 1(1).

Silverman, L. K. (1986) 'The IQ Controversy'. *Roeper Review*, 8(3).

Sisk, D. (1987) *Creative Teaching of Gifted*. McGraw-Hill, New York.

Sports Council (1976) *European 'Sport for All' Charter*. London.

Sports Council (1984) *Annual Report, 1983/84*. London.

Stanley, J. C., Keating, D. and Fox, L. (eds) (1974) *Mathematical Talent: Discovery,Description and Development*. Johns Hopkins University Press, Baltimore, MD.

Sternberg, R. J. (1985) *Beyond IQ. A Triarchic Theory of Human Intelligence.* Cambridge University Press, Cambridge.

Sternberg, R. and Davidson, J. E. (1986) *Conceptions of Giftedness.* Cambridge University Press, Cambridge.

Straker, A. (1983) *Mathematics for Gifted Pupils.* Longman, London.

Tannenbaum, A. J. (1983) *Gifted Children.* Macmillan, London.

Taylor, C. W. (1978) 'How Many Types of Giftedness Can Your Programme Tolerate?' *Journal of Creative Behaviour* 12, 39–51.

Taylor, C. W. (ed.) (1990) *Expanding Awareness of Creative Potentials Worldwide.* Seventh World Conference on Gifted and Talented Children. Trillium Press, New York.

Taylor, R. L. and Sternberg, L. (1989) *Exceptional Children.* Springer-Verlag, New York.

Teare, J. B. (1996a) *A School Policy on Provision for Able Pupils,* 2nd edn. NACE, Northampton.

Teare, J. B. (1996b) *Able Pupils: Practical Identification Strategies.,* 2nd edn. NACE, Northampton.

Tempest, N. R. (1974) *Teaching Clever Children 7–11.* Routledge & Kegan Paul, London.

Terman, L. M. (1981) 'The Discovery and Encouragement of Exceptional Talent'. In W. B. Barbe and J. S. Renzulli (eds), *Psychology and Education of the Gifted,* 3rd edn. John Wiley, New York.

Terman, L. M. and Oden, M. H. (1959) *Genetic Study of Genius: The Gifted Child Grows Up.* Stanford University Press, Stanford, CA.

Tilsley, P. (1979) 'Gifted Children and Their Education'. *Journal of Applied Educational Studies* 8-(1).

Torrance, E. P. (1977) *Discovering and Nurturance of Giftedness in the Culturally Different.* Council for Exceptional Children, Reston, VA.

Torrance, E. P. (1980) 'Assessing the Further Reaches of Creative Potential'. *Journal of Creative Behaviour,* 14, 1–19.

Treffinger, D. J. (1975) 'Teaching for Self-directed Learning: A Priority for the Gifted and Talented'. *Gifted Children Quarterly* 19, 46–59.

Treffinger, D. J. and Renzulli, J. S. (1986) 'Giftedness as Potential for Creative Productivity Transcending IQ Scores'. *Roeper Review,* 8(3), 150–154.

Urban, K. K. (1988) 'Recent Trends in Creativity'. Paper given at ECHA Conference, Zurich.

Urban, K. K. and Jellen, H. G. (1996) *Test for Creative Thinking – Drawing Production.* SWETS Test Services, Lisse, The Netherlands.

Vaughan, M. M. (1977) 'Musical Creativity: Its Cultivation and Measurement'. *Bulletin of Music Education* 50, 72–77.

Vernon, P. E. (1977) *The Psychology and Education of Gifted Children.* Methuen, London.

Wallace, A. (1986) *The Prodigy*. Macmillan, London.

Wallace, B. (1983) *Teaching the Very Able Child*. Ward Lock Educational, London.

Warnock Report (1978) *GB DES Committee of Enquiry into the Education of Handicapped Children and Young People*. HMSO, London.

White, B. L., Kaban, B. T. and Attanucci, J. (1979) *The Origins of Human Competence: The Final Report of the Harvard Pre-school Project*. Lexington Books, Massachusetts.

Whitmore, J. R. (1981) 'Gifted Children with Handicapping Conditions'. *Exceptional Children* 48, 100–114.

Williams, F. E. (1970) *Classroom Ideas for Encouraging Thinking and Teaching*. DOK Publishers, Buffalo, New York.

Willings, D. (1980) *The Creatively Gifted: Recognising and Developing the Creative Personality*. Woodhead Faulkner, Cambridge.

Wittgenstein, L. (1958) *Philosophical Investigations*. Basil Blackwell, Oxford.

Young, P. and Tyre, C. (1992) *Gifted or Able – Realizing Children's Potential*. Open University Press, Milton Keynes.

# Index